Faith Magnified

How to Be Free From Doubt-Aholism

by

Jennifer LeClaire

Psalm 94:19
When doubts filled my mind, your comfort gave me
renewed hope and cheer. NLT

Faith Magnified: How to Be Free From Dout-Aholism.

ISBN - 978-0-9819795-5-7

Copyright © 2013 by Jennifer LeClaire

Published by Jennifer LeClaire

www.jenniferleclaire.org

For easy online ordering visit www.jenniferleclaire.org

DEDICATION

I dedicate this book to my grandmother, Mary Beckett, who always believed in me, never doubted me, and fought the good fight of faith for me long before I ever knew I was in a war. She's now a part of the great cloud of witnesses cheering me on.

CONTENTS

FOREWORD

So many Christians are dying prematurely from cancer and other dreaded diseases. Many appear to have strong faith. Some would question why they died? Others would say, "If they died and they had more faith than me, then maybe faith in the promises of God's Word for healing do not work." That is exactly what the devil tried to do with Job! Doubt and unbelief will cripple your faith. THERE IS A DIABOLICAL PLAN TO CAUSE YOU TO DOUBT GOD. More now than at any other time in history!

Why now? Because this is wrap up of all things. If God can trust you with little things, He is ready to trust you with big things. Jesus is Coming back soon. Sooner than you think! Even a non-believer can see end time events are speeding up! The world is getting darker and darker. It is a demonic, thick darkness. If you do not move forward in God you are deceived. If you are coasting, you are backslidden and dangerously close to deception. When Jesus returns, will He find faith on this earth? More importantly, will He find faith in you?

We are at a crossroads. Those that choose to move forward with God will find themselves entering a new level of glory. You will see the same miracles Jesus demonstrated and even greater. God speaks of this distinction in Isaiah 60:1-3 (AMP): "ARISE [from the depression and prostration in which circumstances have kept you—rise to a new life]! Shine (be radiant with the glory of the Lord), for your light has come, and the glory of the Lord has risen upon you! For behold, darkness shall cover the earth, and dense darkness [all] peoples, but the Lord shall arise upon you, and His glory shall be seen on you. And nations shall come to your light, and kings to the brightness of your rising."

Jennifer LeClaire has been trained in the school of the Holy Spirit as a forerunner to be an example of the new normal. I doubt if many true believers will survive when our money fails, war is on our shores and diseases that man cannot cure hit UNLESS they operate in true bible faith. It will not be your stored food and gold that will be the difference maker. Without faith you cannot please God. You are created to move in great faith. Jennifer's teaching removes the little foxes that spoil the vine and prepares you for the greatest adventure in history. You will not only survive but you will thrive.

Sid Roth
Its Supernatural/Messianic Vision

PREFACE

Doubtaholism. What a concept, eh? The Holy Spirit gave me this attention-getting twist on the issue of doubt and unbelief a few years ago as I was preparing a Christian living column for an international Christian magazine that seeks to advance Christian life and culture. The purpose of the column is to address the challenges Christians face in every day life, both spiritual and natural, with a biblical response.

Oftentimes, the lessons I share in these columns come from my own life. I tend to study to live rather than study to write or to teach. So when you read my Christian living articles you are discovering the practical lessons I learned in the midst of my own struggles and victories. Notice I say victories. Thanks be to God, who always causes us to triumph in Christ and makes manifest the aroma of His knowledge to us in every place (2 Corinthians 2:14). Amen?

The concept of "Dealing with Doubtaholism" was first an article in the magazine, but the Holy Spirit had so much more to say than I could fit in a 900-word column. It's been years now since I first penned the article on which this book is based. But I believe now is the time to distribute a more in-depth body of work on the topic of doubt, its dangers, and how to resist it in Christ. It's vital that we prepare our hearts to receive everything God has for us in our personal lives, our families, our ministries and the Church at large. That preparation means rooting out doubt that dilutes our faith. In doing so, I believe we will come away with greater discernment in every area of our lives – and greater faith.

If you've picked up this book, there's a pretty good chance you discern a struggle with doubt in your own soul. Don't let the voice of doubt rob from you any longer! The devil will assuredly fight you on your journey to rid yourself of "doubtaholism." He may already be trying to convince you that you don't have a problem with doubt or that this book can't help you. That's the voice of doubt itself. Resist it actively as you read the pages ahead.

Listen, no condemnation. Doubt is sneaky and it plagues us all to some degree or we'd be walking in the fullness of God, believing in our heart and confessing with our mouths and seeing 100 percent of God's promises manifesting in our lives 100 percent of the time. While we aren't yet mature enough to handle some of the things God has in store for us, we need to be of this mind: If there is something God wants me to have right now, then I want it right now! I refuse to let doubt stand in the way of fulfilling His destiny for me.

How about you? If you are ready to come into greater levels of faith, then let the Holy Spirit guide you through this 12-step program for dealing with doubtaholism. You'll walk away with more prayer answers, more peace and more freedom in Christ.

I HAVE A WHAT?
I DON'T BELIEVE IT!

Watch how God works. You might find my testimony ironic, but I am here to tell you it's absolutely miraculous how God works all things together for good to those who love Him and are called according to His purpose (Romans 8:28).

The story begins shortly after I enrolled in Rhema Correspondence Bible School some years ago. I couldn't make it to Tulsa because I was already serving on staff at a South Florida church, as well as managing several businesses. But I wanted to get the solid faith foundation Kenneth E. Hagin brought to the Body of Christ. I wanted a regimented study program that would keep me on a steady diet of faith teachings I could grow on.

The curriculum, of course, begins with studies on faith, what it is and how it works. I tell you, the Holy Spirit used the biblical truth in Dr. Hagin's books to open my eyes about how to walk in faith at a much greater level. The writings were clear and simple. The anecdotes were colorful and memorable. And the anointing seemed to cause black ink to jump off the white pages that hosted them and into my hungry spirit. Indeed, the Word of faith demanded the attention of heart and the battle with my soul was on.

The Skirmish Between Soul and Spirit

Dr. Hagin taught that you can believe in your heart and yet still struggle with doubt coming against your soul. Let me tell you, sometimes that struggle is more than a skirmish between soul and spirit. Sometimes it seems like World War III. If you keep meditating on the Word of God and praying in the Spirit as you stand on the battlefield and fight for the promises of God, your heart will win out. But if you don't understand how to fight that battle, your soul will cave in to doubt's pressure and your prayers will go unanswered because God only responds to faith.

Back then I didn't even understand I was in a battle. All I knew was this: There was something terribly wrong. I was studying faith diligently and intensely and instead of walking in a new dimension of believing and receiving I was left wondering. Wondering why my prayers weren't answered. Wondering why everything around me seemed to be falling apart. Wondering why this truth wasn't working for me. What I didn't realize was that the enemy kicked the spiritual warfare up a few notches because he knew a rhema would make me unstoppable. He was opposing this revelation in my life. Doubt and unbelief was at play behind the scenes but I didn't recognize it. A spirit of unbelief was hindering me. I was blind to it. I was deceived.

Casting Out Devils

When you hit a wall you can't knock down, climb over or dig your way under, you need to humble yourself and get some help from your elders. I didn't know what was the matter with me, but I knew I couldn't break through on my own. I did what most people in our local church do: I counseled with the prophetic minister in my church. She flowed in a spirit of counsel and is also a deliverance minister that devils loathe to see coming. While I can't remember what we talked about anymore, I do remember that it wasn't anything about faith or doubt. I was rehearsing a whiney tale about how frustrated I was with the circumstances of my life in the midst of my pursuit of faith revelations.

The prophetic minister listened for about 60 seconds. That's because that's about how long it took her to discern what was going on. With authority and compassion in her voice, she said six words to me that were shocking and unexpected: "You have a spirit of unbelief."

I thought to myself, "I have a what? I don't believe it!" Of course, I never actually voiced those thoughts. The truth of the matter was I did believe her in my heart. I had built a trust with her and had witnessed Jesus set many people free from the bondage of Satan's lies through her ministry.

As she sat across from me in silence waiting for a response, those same thoughts repeated like a skipping CD, "No way. I don't believe this." And in those thoughts lay the confirmation. Right then and there I saw the enemy's assignment. That devilish spirit was speaking to me even then, cajoling me with unbelief because it didn't want to flee from the stronghold it had expertly built in my soul. But it was that very spirit that was watering down my faith and frustrating me so.

So herein lies the irony. I had been studying faith faithfully while doubt and unbelief was holding me in bondage to its lies. My will was aligned with God, but there was a raging battle in my mind and emotions. But watch how God works: As I diligently studied His Word, faith squeezed that unbelief to the surface. The Word of faith was chipping away at the adversaries of my soul. I flooded that spirit of unbelief with the word of truth and by the time prophetic minister came in, it was cornered. The Bible says, "But if I with the finger of God cast out devils, no doubt the kingdom of God is come upon you" (Luke 11:20). No doubt is right! That spirit of unbelief had no choice but to leave because I renounced it in the name of Jesus.

I believe that spirit of unbelief was on its way out the door already and, with or without a deliverance minister, the truth that I walked in would have set me free sooner or later. But I was left wondering, how did that spirit of unbelief get hold of me in the first place? What was the doorway?

Chapter 2

DOUBT: THE DOORWAY TO UNBELIEF

"Doubt is the doorway to unbelief." When I heard the Holy Spirit speak those words, I began to ponder the danger of doubt. I understood that it was doubt that let that spirit of unbelief erect a stronghold in my soul.

Doubt is uncertainty but God's Word is certain.

> God is not a man that He should lie; neither the son of man that He should repent: hath He said, and shall He not do it? or hath He spoken, and shall He not make it good? (Numbers 23:19)

Let God be true, but every man a liar – and not only every many but every spirit that is not of God. Satan is the Father of lies, and the fallen angels – including the spirits of doubt and unbelief – are carrying out his wicked plots.

When the Holy Spirit revealed to me doubt is the doorway to unbelief I began to see doubt as more than just a mindset that prevents us from casting the proverbial mountain into the sea. I began to see doubt as a spiritual disease whose goal is to cripple our Christian lives. I dub this disease doubtaholism.

Doubt is a cousin of fear and suspicion that blocks faith and discernment. To doubt is to lack confidence in the Word of God. Doubt is failing to fully trust in the Lord Jesus Christ. Just like alcohol, doubt is a depressant. It damages our heart, lowers our resistance to infection, and leaves us impotent. Just like alcohol, doubt impairs our judgment, brings fatigue and leaves a nasty hangover all its own. Just like alcoholism, chronic doubt impairs our learning ability, disorients us, and causes mental confusion.

Redeemed from the Curse of the Law

In Deuteronomy 28:66, we learn that doubt is part of the curse of the law: "Your life shall hang in doubt before you; day and night you shall be worried, and have no assurance of your life." Thank God Jesus came to redeem us from the curse of the law. Here's more good news: While alcohol withdrawal can cause tremors and convulsions, withdrawing from doubt causes freedom and liberty in Christ. Hallelujah!

In His wisdom, God has made it easy for us. He spelled it all out in black, white and red. Prophets and apostles of old wrote down what He said so we would know His will in all things. We also have chronicles of the lives of faith heroes who stumbled now and again to show us practical lessons for how to avoid the enemy's pitfalls.

Jesus has given us apostles, prophets, evangelists, pastors and teachers to equip us with the Word. Modern technology makes it possible to listen to the Word at night while we sleep, look up Scriptures on the Internet with a few keystrokes, and fly around the world to receive impartations from men and women of God. Let's not forget Christian TV and radio.

Here's my point: We have no excuse to doubt or disbelief Him. We can hear the Word in multiple mediums. If God had not given us the ingredients to build faith, we could call Him unjust. But He is not unjust. He has given us the ingredients and even told us how to mix them. Faith comes by hearing, and hearing by the Word of God (Romans 10:17). It's up to us to do our part instead of being like Doubting Thomas who had to see with his eyes before he would dare to believe.

Dangerous Questions

In elementary school, my daughter was required to take a series of classes known as D.A.R.E. The acronym stands for Drug Abuse Resistance Education. She learned the skills she needed to avoid involvement in drugs, gangs and violence. She learned how to resist peer pressure and live a drug-free life. Part of that training was outlining the danger of drugs and the devastating path drug use takes people down.

It's only appropriate for you to see for yourself in the Word of God how dangerous doubt really is. The Bible has plenty to say about it, and you need to know it so you can fight it off like the demonic power it is. Once you learn to resist doubt, you can receive God's best for your life.

> **Doubting is a sin you don't want to practice because it leads to the death of your dreams.**

You remember Jesus' sermon about worry? He was talking about natural needs, like clothing and food and drink. In Luke 12:29, Jesus told His disciples not "be doubtful of mind." He also offered some advice for those who were doubtful of mind: Seek the Kingdom. If you find yourself doubtful of mind, seek the Kingdom perspective. It's a command, not a suggestion.

Doubting is a sin you don't want to practice because it leads to the death of your dreams.

Remember, the Israelites who doubted God died in the wilderness? God has a better plan for you. But you must believe.

Doubt can also leave you prey to a religious spirit. Remember when the Jesus walked in the temple in Solomon's porch? The Jews gathered around Him and said,

> "How long are You going to keep us in doubt and suspense? If You are really the Christ (the Messiah), tell us so plainly and openly. Jesus answered them, I have told you so, yet you do not believe Me [you do not trust Me and rely on Me]" (John 10:23-25 AMP).

The Jews took up stones with the intent of murdering Jesus because He told them the truth – and because they doubted His veracity.

What about you? Do you believe Jesus – the living Word of God? Do you trust and rely on Him and not on your own understanding? Our own understanding often doubts what we don't readily understand. It's easier to believe the reasonable than the impossible, yet Jesus said all things are possible to him who believes – not to him who understands and certainly not to him who doubts. Doubt disqualifies you from the manifested dream.

Here's the problem: We tend to read the Bible through the lens of what we've already been taught or experienced rather than what it truly means. In other words, we often read what we believe rather than believing what we read. If what we read doesn't match what we already believe, doubt finds a crack to seep through. (That's why it's so important who you let feed you spiritual food.) Religion causes us to continually "learn" but never come to the knowledge of the truth. (2 Timothy 3:7). When we doubt God means just exactly what He says He means in His Word, the religious spirit stands ready to lead us into doubt and unbelief. What lens are you looking through? Selah.

Faith Cometh, Doubt Killeth

Faith comes by hearing. So if you are doubting, you have to ask yourself: What am I hearing? In other words, what are you giving ear to? Are you listening to the still small voice of God in the matter, or are you listening to the circumstances screaming at your soul? Are you listening to the Holy Spirit or some other spirit? We have to guard our hearts with all diligence because out it flow the issues of life (Proverbs 4:23). Out of our heart also flows the faith that puts the creative force behind our confession. When faith comes, it brings peace, joy, revelation, determination and other godly manifestations. When doubt comes, it brings fear, confusion, stress and other ungodly manifestations.

After Jesus was resurrected, some of the disciples were going to a village called Emmaus when Jesus joined them and talked openly with them about the Christ. He called them foolish and slow of heart to believe what the prophets had spoken and what the Scriptures revealed (Luke 24:13-33). These two disciples didn't realize it was Jesus until He departed from them, but when they got the revelation that the risen Christ was among them they returned to Jerusalem and told the 11 remaining Apostles of the Lamb that the Lord had risen. Suddenly, Jesus showed up in their midst.

> "But the whole group was startled and frightened, thinking they were seeing a ghost! 'Why are you frightened?' he asked. 'Why are your hearts filled with doubt? Look at my hands. Look at my feet. You can see that it's really me. Touch me and make sure that I am not a ghost, because ghosts don't have bodies, as you see that I do'."
> Luke 24:37-39 NLT

Can you see how doubt led to fear? The disciples feared because they thought Jesus was an evil spirit, a devil, or some ghost other than the Holy Ghost whom had been promised but not yet sent. Kahil Gibran, a Lebanese writer and artist who lived in the early 1900s, had an interesting perspective on fear. He said this: "Fear of the devil is one way of doubting God."

That's a true statement because fear of the devil – or fear of the circumstances he likes to magnify in attempts to cloud the eyes of faith for that matter – demonstrates a lack of trust in God's preserving power.

David confronted fear eyeball to eyeball many times. Instead of doubting His God, he spoke the opposite of fear out of his mouth. He spoke faith:

> "Preserve my life, for I am godly and dedicated; O my God, save Your servant, for I trust in You [leaning and believing on You, committing all and confidently looking to You, without fear or doubt]" (Psalm 86:2 AMP).

I like this, and it reminds me of something President Abraham Lincoln, the great liberator, once said: "Better to remain silent and be thought a fool than to speak out and remove all doubt." It's better to remain silent and let the devil think you're a fool if you can't offer a faith-filled confession that's pleasing to God. But it's oh so much better to speak out the Word and in doing so build up your faith and remove all doubt.

Beyond the Shadow of a Doubt

Doubt's ultimate goal is to prevent you from receiving from God. Doubt causes many people to spend eternity in hell. Doubt even causes many Christians to live below their means, stressed instead of blessed, because they don't have the peace of mind that comes with putting their trust in the living God. Doubt blocks your prayer answers and sets you up to have

an evil heart of unbelief that causes you to wander around in the wilderness instead of walking into the Promised Land.

God is willing to give you the desires of your heart if you are merely willing to believe beyond the shadow of a doubt. Have you ever thought about where that cliché – beyond the shadow of a doubt – came from? If an issue is beyond the very shadow that doubt casts, that means absolutely no doubt remains. It is far enough from doubt that even doubt's shadow does not touch it.

Consider this: The sun and light bulbs give off light. When something blocks that light, it creates a shadow. In light of that truth, consider Merriam-Webster's definition of doubt:

> a partial darkness or obscurity within
> a part of space from which rays from
> a source of light are cut off by an
> interposed opaque body; an imperfect
> or faint representation; an imitation
> of something; a reflected image; a
> source of gloom or unhappiness.

Doubt's shadow reflects an image alright, but it's the opposite image of truth. It's an imperfect representation of what the Word says. Doubt's shadow casts gloom over our faith and leads us to unhappiness – and unbelief.

There's joy in believing (John 16:24). God's Word is a lamp unto our feet. When the voice of the enemy, negative circumstances, nay sayers, or our own impatience in waiting for the prayer answer rises up to block that light, we fall prey to the dangers of doubt and ultimately unbelief. Healing Evangelist F.F. Bosworth once said, "Believe your beliefs and not your doubts." Therein lies the key.

Chapter 3

WHY AREN'T MY PRAYERS ANSWERED?

I needed a healing. I had several "medical conditions" in my physical body that manifested in a string of strange ways. The root of it was a whacked out sympathetic nervous system that caused my heart to beat too fast and my blood pressure to rise up to the point that I would become too dizzy to stand. I was taking medications for this "condition" for which there was no cure, and the medications, of course, caused more unwanted symptoms. I needed a healing.

When I got saved, someone told me God could heal people. They told me testimonies of seeing limbs grow out of stubs, blind eyes opening, and other miraculous works. They told me of ministers like Binny Hinn and Oral Roberts. They told me healing is for today. I decided to give it a try. (That was my first mistake. You don't give God's Word your best shot. You give it your heart.) I asked God to heal me. Nothing happened. I went to the church to have the elders lay hands on me. Nothing happened. I drove 300 miles to attend a Binny Hinn conference, determined to get my healing. Nothing happened. (Determination alone won't deliver results. You have to believe from your heart and speak with your mouth over and over again.)

I needed a healing, but all I wound up with was disappointment and that disappointment led me into the death grips of doubt. The devil really had a heyday in my mind. He filled my head with all sorts of doubt; doubts about the truth of healing for today, doubts about God's ability to heal this rare "condition," even doubts about my own salvation. Once you entertain one doubt, you invite a ballroom with guests like uncertainty, misgivings, qualms, distrust, suspicion, skepticism and, of course, unbelief. It's time to crash the party with your faith and send those rascals home so you can see God move in your life.

Breaking Doubt's Vicious Cycle

My healing testimony is one example of how the doubting devil sets us up: If you've been praying for the same thing for years and you haven't received an answer, or if your prayer-answer-track-record is poor, then it gets harder and harder to believe that God wants to answer you the next time you pray. The devil introduces doubtful disputations to your mind. It becomes a vicious cycle that only faith can break.

As Bosworth said, 'believe your beliefs and not your doubts.' But make sure you're believing God's Word without wavering. There have been mountains of books written on mountain-moving faith. We won't review all those truths here. What I want you to see in this section is why your prayers ultimately go unanswered.

Assuming you are asking (the Bible says you have not because you ask not) and assuming you aren't asking so you can consume it upon your lusts, and assuming you are praying in line with God's will, the reason you are not getting prayer answers is because you are believing your doubts instead of believing your beliefs. You are believing the circumstances instead of believing the Word of God. You are believing what you see with your eyes rather than what you hear by the Word. Maybe you don't even know what the Word says about your situation, so you don't have a Scripture to hang your faith on in prayer. If we pray according to God's will, we know that He hears us and we can believe that He will answer us (1 John 5:14-15). Doubt comes in when we aren't sure what the will of God is.

> "Believe your beliefs and not your doubts."
> Bosworth

Your prayers aren't getting answered because you are wavering from faith to doubt to unbelief to fear to faith to doubt to unbelief to fear – it's that vicious cycle we talked about earlier. It can only be broken by unwavering faith. Faith that refuses to doubt God's Word no matter what your physical body or your soul screams. What forces the devil to flee? Faith that arises from your spirit because you've sowed the Word in your heart and spoken it out of your mouth with conviction.

> "If any of you is deficient in wisdom, let him ask of the giving God [Who gives] to everyone liberally and ungrudgingly, without reproaching or faultfinding, and it will be given him. Only it must be in faith that he asks with no wavering (no hesitating, no doubting). For the one who wavers (hesitates, doubts) is like the billowing surge out at sea that is blown hither and thither and tossed by the wind. For truly, let not such a person imagine that he will receive anything [he asks for] from the Lord." (James 1:5-7, AMP)

I like this verse. You could put any Bible promise in place of the word "wisdom" in that verse and it would still ring true. If any of you lack – provision. If any of you lack – healing. If any of you lack – peace. If any of you lack – whatever you lack God is willing to provide all of your needs according to His riches in glory by Christ Jesus. But He doesn't respond to your needs. And He certainly doesn't respond to your doubts. He responds to your unwavering faith. The storms will come, but they won't blow you hither and thither if your faith is unwavering. If you don't doubt God's Word in whatever storm you find yourself in, you can simply cast the care, take care of your responsibility in the matter, and take a nap like Jesus did (Matthew 8:23-27).

Doubt Will Destroy Your Prayer Life

The Apostle Paul used doubt and wrath in the same breath when he gave his spiritual son Timothy instructions for godly behavior. "I desire therefore that in every place men should pray, without anger or quarreling or resentment or doubt [in their minds], lifting up holy hands" (1 Timothy 2:5-9 AMP). Resentment, quarrelling and anger will hinder your prayer life – but doubt will destroy it.

You don't have to take my word for it, but you do have to take the Word for it. Jesus said,

> "Whosoever shall say unto this mountain, Be thou removed, and be thou cast into the sea; and shall not doubt in his heart, but shall believe that those things which he saith

shall come to pass; he shall have whatsoever he saith" (Mark 11:23).

Would it be fair, then, to read it this way: Whosoever shall say unto this mountain, Be thou removed, and be thou cast into the sea; but shall doubt in his heart, and not believe that those things which he saith shall come to pass; he shall not have whatsoever he saith. Indeed, it is fair. That's the message Jesus is trying to get across. You've got to belief you've got it before you get it. But if you doubt you've got it – if you're like Doubting Thomas and demand to see it before you believe it – you'll never get it.

> **You've got to believe you've got it before you get it.**

It's been said that doubt makes the mountain that faith can move. But why create a mountain of doubt to begin with? Doubts will come, but why use it as evidence to build a case against the Word of God? Faith is the evidence of things hoped for, and your expectation shall not be cut off (Proverbs 23:18). If you believe you receive and refuse to back down from what the Word says, you will see the promise manifest.

I finally did receive my healing. Do you want to know how? It wasn't in a prayer line; it wasn't by calling the elders to anoint me with oil and pray for me. There's nothing wrong with having a point of contact with God and I encourage the laying on of hands. But that's not how I got my healing. It wasn't from a conference. It wasn't from a TV show.

I got my healing by meditating on what the Word of God says about healing. By confessing healing Scriptures out of my very own mouth. By praying in the Spirit to build up my most holy faith. By pleading the blood of Jesus. By thanking God that His Word is true. By faith and patience. And, at the same time, by casting down imaginations when symptoms would arise. By binding up those symptoms in the name of Jesus. By resisting the devil. By fighting the power of doubt and unbelief until the devil got so tired of hearing the truth come out of my mouth that he fled seven ways. Ha! You can do the same.

Build up your faith in whatever area you are believing for before you pray. Get that truth in you solidly before you release your prayer. Then stand on His Word and defy doubt. Whatever things you ask for in prayer, believing, you will receive (Matthew 21:22).

Doubt Versus Discernment

Before we move on to the next chapter, I want to clear up a question I know the devil will use to give you an excuse to doubt. When we talk about doubt, we are talking about not doubting God's Word. That doesn't mean that we throw discernment out the window when a preacher is preaching the Word, teacher is teaching the Word, or a prophet is prophesying a prophetic word.

Failing to study the Word of God for yourself will leave you without the discernment to recognize false teachings and false prophecies when you hear them. If you put your faith in a false prophecy or a false interpretation of the Word, then you could open yourself up to a slew of errors as you build wrong belief systems on wrong utterances. It's like building a house on a foundation with defective materials. There's bound to be problems down the road – eventually.

We Should Have Consulted God!

Remember Joshua and his encounter with the inhabitants of Gibeon? The people of Gibeon heard how Joshua utterly defeated Jericho and Ai and cooked up a ruse. They posed as travelers: their donkeys loaded with patched sacks and mended wineskins, threadbare sandals on their feet, tattered clothes on their bodies, nothing but dry crusts and crumbs for food. They came to Joshua at Gilgal and told Joshua the had come from a far land and wanted to make a covenant. Well, Joshua should have inquired of the Lord but instead he was quick to believe their story.

On the surface, who could blame him? The circumstances appeared authentic:

"They posed as travelers: their donkeys loaded with patched sacks and mended wineskins, threadbare sandals on their feet, tattered clothes on their bodies, nothing but dry crusts and crumbs for food" (Joshua 9:4-5, The Message).

Their story was convincing: Those manipulative Gibeonites told Joshua that they had come from a far-off country. They told Joshua they came because they heard such great things about Jehovah God and all the things He did in Egypt. Let's listen in:

"This bread was warm from the oven when we packed it and left to come and see you. Now look at it—crusts and crumbs. And our cracked and mended wineskins, good as new when we filled them. And our clothes and sandals, in tatters from the long, hard traveling. The men of Israel looked them over and accepted the evidence. But they didn't ask God about it." (Joshua 9:12-14, The Message)

The Gibeonites told a bold-faced lie. And because Israel's leaders made a covenant with them, they couldn't attack Gibeon and take dominion in that area. (Joshua 9). If they had asked God, He would have revealed the deception but instead they walked into it based on what their natural eyes and ears saw and heard.

Joshua wasn't the first to lack discernment in the face of deception. Eve should have doubted the serpent's tall tale. She should have fallen back on what God said rather than entertaining the you-can-be-just-like-God story the devil concocted (Genesis 3:1-5). Like Joshua, she didn't consult with God. There are many examples of Bible characters that should have doubted what they heard. Remember the man of God who took instruction from the old prophet and got killed by a lion (1 Kings 13:11-18)? How about Naaman? He should have doubted Gehazi.

So we see there is a time to doubt, but never in the face of God's Word. Remember, if you can believe it you can have it. If you let doubt lead you into unbelief, you won't get it. So let's take a look at unbelief's agenda in the next chapter.

Chapter 4

UNDERSTANDING UNBELIEF'S AGENDA

Unbelief's primary agenda is to send people straight to hell for all eternity. It's the belief in our hearts and confession with our mouths that Jesus died on a cross for the sin of the world and was raised from the dead by the power of God after three days that affords us salvation. Not by works, lest any man should boast (Ephesians 2:10). Faith alone – belief in God's Word – delivers us, heals us, and saves us... Unbelief, by contrast, binds us, oppresses us and ultimately destroys us.

Once you've accepted Jesus as your Lord and Savior and are pursuing His plan for your life, the unbelief's assignment evolves. The agenda then is to keep you from walking in the fullness of the more than 7,000 promises in He made in His Word. Unbelief is a thief. It will rob the blessings of God from you and will try to use you as a vehicle to rob God's blessings from others. Indeed, unbelief is the mortal sin.

Let's go back to the Garden of Eden. I have read the account many times and indeed there are many layers of revelation to be discovered, many mysteries to be revealed. But as I was studying one day, the Holy Spirit suddenly showed me unbelief's agenda in the Garden. Let's listen in to the historical account of the fall of man – because of unbelief.

"The serpent was the shrewdest of all the wild animals the Lord God had made. One day he asked the woman, 'Did God really say you must not eat the fruit from any of the trees in the garden?' Of course we may eat fruit from the trees in the garden,' the woman replied. 'It's only the fruit from the tree in the middle of the garden that we are not allowed to eat. God said, 'You must not eat it or even touch it; if you do, you will die'."

> 'You won't die!' the serpent replied to the woman. 'God knows that your eyes will be opened as soon as you eat it, and you will be like God, knowing both good and evil.' The woman was convinced. She saw that the tree was beautiful and its fruit looked delicious, and she wanted the wisdom it would give her. So she took some of the fruit and ate it.

Then she gave some to her husband,
who was with her, and he ate it, too."
(Genesis 3:1-6)

Doubt, Deception and Disobedience

Notice the serpent launched out with doubt. The
serpent didn't come to Eve with a shiny piece of fruit
in his hand and invite her to sample it. That's because
the serpent needed her to understand the choice she
was making. The serpent, in order to cause man to sin,
had to get man to willfully and disobey God's Word.
Tricking her by giving her fruit from the Tree of the
Knowledge of Good and Evil without her knowing
its source wouldn't do the trick.

In other words, it wasn't that the Tree of
Knowledge of Good and Evil contained some magic
potion that activated spiritual death when Eve and
Adam partook. We're not talking about the Wicked
Witch in Snow White and the Seven Dwarves, who
tricked the beloved Disney matron into taking a bite
of a poison apple that caused her to fall into a deep
sleep. We're talking about a clever devil that knows
doubt is the doorway to unbelief.

So the serpent launched out with doubt: "Did
God really say you must not eat the fruit from
any of the trees in the garden?" Eve corrected the
devil's perversion right away, clarifying – and by
clarifying acknowledging her understanding of the
commandment – that God only prohibited them

from eating of the fruit from the tree in the middle of the garden. Eve did what Jesus did in the wilderness. She gave Him the Word of God on the matter: "God said, 'You must not eat it or even touch it; if you do, you will die'."

The serpent's response, in essence: "God's lying to you about that tree. You won't die if you eat from it. In fact, not only will you not die, you will be just like Him when you eat it." Just that quick, the woman was convinced. It didn't take the devil a week to talk her into it. The Bible doesn't record a long theological debate between Eve and the serpent. The Bible doesn't record a struggle in Eve's soul over what she should do. The serpent had introduced doubt of God's Word into Eve's mind with his questioning, and because she entertained it, the door to unbelief was opened wide enough for her to walk through.

Eve's sin was unbelief. She walked through the door of unbelief with seemingly little hesitation. She cannot even claim ignorance. She spoke God's Word out of her own mouth. The bottom line is this: Eve chose to believe what the devil said instead of what God said. And she must have felt pretty good about her decision at first. When she ate the fruit, she didn't drop dead. In her mind that must have proved the serpent's point. She didn't seem to hesitate to offer the forbidden fruit to her husband. And he ate it, too. I can only imagine the spiritual battle in that Garden must have been intense. The demonic pressure...the tempting spirits…the imaginations. But Eve made a choice to believe the devil over God.

Like Eve, we have a will and faith is a choice. We can choose to believe God's Word no matter what we see or hear. Or we can choose to believe what we see or hear over God's Word. The concept is really that simple. It's not as easy to walk out sometimes, especially when the spiritual battle intensifies. But Greater is He who is in us than He who is in the world (1 John 4:4). We have an advantage, in some sense, over Eve. We have 4,000 years of biblical history to rely on. We have chronicles of how the devil works. We have great men and women of God with personal experiences to share that are relevant to every day life. We don't have to walk through the doorway of doubt down the corridor of unbelief. Hallelujah!

Unbelief: The Opposite of Faith

Just as we looked at the danger of doubt, there is an unbelievable end to unbelief. Unbelief prevented even Jesus from doing the Father's will in His hometown. (God is always willing to heal but unbelief ties His hands.) Unbelief hindered the disciples from casting a devil out of a boy. Unbelief caused the Israelites to wander around in the desert for 40 years – and unbelief caused millions to die there without entering into the Promised Land.

What is unbelief? Miriam-Webster's definition hits the nail on the head: Incredulity or skepticism, especially in matters of religious faith. It's often been said that fear is the opposite of faith or that sight is the opposite of faith. I won't dispute that. But if you want a proper antonym, unbelief is the opposite of faith. Faith is belief and trust in and loyalty to God. Unbelief is rejecting God's Word as untrue. We can't sugar coat unbelief. The truth is we are always believing something. We are either believing God's report or believing the devil's report.

Let's look at what the Bible has to say about unbelief. Remember when Jesus went to His own country of Nazareth?

> "He taught in their synagogue so that they were amazed with bewildered wonder, and said, Where did this Man get this wisdom and these miraculous powers? Is not this the carpenter's Son? Is not His mother called Mary? And are not His brothers James and Joseph and Simon and Judas? And do not all His sisters live here among us? Where then did this Man get all this?" (Matthew 13:55-56 AMP).

Jesus' fellow Nazarenes reasoned in their minds. That reasoning lead to doubt, and that doubt lead to unbelief. More than that, the Bible says they took offense at Him. Offense is a spirit the devil uses to rob us from receiving from authority figures in our life. You thought the pastor was ignoring you last Sunday morning before church because he walked by without saying hello. You reasoned it out in your mind until you finally fell for Satan's bait of offence. Now, instead of an expecting spirit and ears to hear the Sunday sermon, you are offended and hindered from receiving what God has for you.

The Amplified Bible says, "He did not do many works of power there, because of their unbelief (their lack of faith in the divine mission of Jesus)" (Matthew 13:58). Unbelief is a lack of faith in the divine mission of the Jesus (the Word).

> We can't sugar coat unbelief. The truth is we are always believing something.

What is the divine mission of the Word? To save you, to heal you, to equip you, to prosper you, to deliver you, to teach you, to send you…you get the picture. What we need to understand is there is a demonic assignment called unbelief laying wait to thwart that divine mission in our lives. God wants to do miracles in your life, but He needs you to take Him at His Word. Jesus said, "Only believe" (Mark 5:36). Faith gets your prayers answered. Unbelief voids them.

When I was a kid, our teachers ingrained a certain spelling trick into our little moldable brains that I still remember. It goes like this: "I before E except after C." But I had another teacher who taught us another spelling trick that, in retrospect, is devilish. She said, "There's a 'lie' in 'believe'." I remember at the time thinking that was practically impossible, and that's why it was so easy to remember. But the Holy Ghost has helped me redeem that old spelling trick to the glory of Jesus. I like to remember it this way: There's a lie in unbelief. When we aren't believing God's Word, it's because we are believing a lie. There's always a lie in unbelief. If you can uncover the lie, you can renew your mind and get to believing again.

Chapter 5

THE THIEF NAMED 'LITTLE FAITH'

The Bible talks about contrasting types of faith: great faith and little faith. One is free from doubt and one is mixed with doubt. While every man is given the measure of faith (Romans 12:3) it's up to the receiver to shut the door on doubtful disputations that attempt to dilute its power. Yes, faith has power – the power to pull what you are hoping for into existence. Let's look at a few Scriptural translations of Hebrews 11:1. We need to get an understanding of what faith is before we can discern between great and little faith in our own hearts.

> Now faith is the substance of things hoped for, the evidence of things not seen (King James).

Now faith is being sure of what we hope for and certain of what we do not see. (New International Version).

Now faith is a well-grounded assurance of that for which we hope, and a conviction of the reality of things which we do not see (Weymouth).

Faith is the confidence that what we hope for will actually happen; it gives us assurance about things we cannot see (New Living Translation).

It's our handle on what we can't see. The act of faith is what distinguished our ancestors, set them above the crowd (The Message).

Now Faith is the assurance (the confirmation, the title deed) of the things [we] hope for, being the proof of things [we] do not see and the conviction of their reality [faith perceiving as real fact what is not revealed to the senses] (Amplified).

So we see from these various translations that faith is a substance, it's evidence, it's a certainty, a well-grounded assurance, a conviction of reality, a confidence, a handle, a title deed, a confirmation and proof. This is great faith, the faith of God. Great faith puts a demand on the Word of God and pulls it into existence. Great faith brings God's intangible, abstract promises into tangible reality. Great faith settles a matter.

By contrast, little faith is mixed with doubt. Doubt comes from the Latin word "dubious." When you doubt, you lack confidence in something. Little faith distrusts. Little faith considers it unlikely. Little faith leaves room for opinions. Little faith is uncertainty of belief that interferes with decision-making. Little faith is an inclination not to believe or accept something. Can you see the difference between great faith and little faith?

I can hear the voice of religion right now. It's quoting this Scripture: "If ye have faith as a grain of mustard seed, ye shall say unto this mountain, Remove hence to yonder place; and it shall remove; and nothing shall be impossible unto you" (Matthew 17:20). Well, I asked the Lord about that.

If you put that Scripture in context, you'll see that Jesus' words came in response to a question from His disciples. They wanted to know why they couldn't cast a demon out of a little boy. Jesus told them it was because of their unbelief. The NIV Bible translates unbelief in that verse to read, "because you have so little faith."

Well, isn't a grain of mustard seed little? Doesn't the Bible say all we need is faith the size of a grain of mustard seed in order to move a mountain? If I have faith the size of a little grain of mustard seed, isn't that enough? Yes, the Lord told me, but only if that faith is pure. Great faith is pure faith. Little faith is mixed with doubt, unbelief or fear.

It doesn't take a lot of faith to receive any promise from God. It just requires pure faith in your heart. Even if there's a battle in your mind, you can have pure faith in your heart that will win the battle in your mind and receive what you've got pure faith for.

Little Faith Robs Your Provision

Let's take a look at some incidents in the Bible where Jesus corrected people for having little faith. What you'll notice is having "little faith" isn't a good thing in the Lord's eyes. Why? Again, it's because little faith isn't pure faith. It's mixed with doubt.

In one Bible scene we have an account in which Jesus' disciples were clearly worried about what they would eat and what they would drink. They were concerned about what they would wear. Jesus told them to consider the fowls of the air, which neither sow nor reap yet receive what they need to live. He pointed to the lilies of the field, and noted that they don't toil or spin but the are arrayed in finer style than King Solomon in all his glory.

> Then Jesus said, "Wherefore, if God
> so clothe the grass of the field, which
> to day is, and tomorrow is cast into the
> oven, shall he not much more clothe you,
> O ye of little faith?" (Matthew 6:30)

If the disciples had pure faith, they wouldn't have taken thought of what they should eat or what they should drink or how they would afford new clothes. Those aren't concerns of covenant people. Jehovah Jireh provides more than enough of everything we need to live – if we believe. Our job is to seek first the Kingdom of God and His righteousness. He'll take care of the rest. But little faith questions whether God will do it for you. He may do it for the birds and the grass, but will He do it for you? Little faith robs your provision because it doubts the Provider.

Little Faith Discounts God's Power

Another time, Jesus' disciples followed Him into a ship. It wasn't long before a great tempest arose in the sea, insomuch that the ship was covered with the waves. Jesus was sound asleep.

> "And his disciples came to him, and
> awoke him, saying, Lord, save us:
> we perish. And he saith unto them,
> Why are ye fearful, O ye of little
> faith? Then he arose, and rebuked

the winds and the sea; and there was
a great calm (Matthew 8:25-26).

Remember, Jesus got into the boat and they
followed Him. What were His disciples thinking?
That Jesus led them out to sea to die a horrid death?
These men had seen Jesus perform many mighty
miracles at this point, but they still doubted His power.
After Jesus rebuked the disciples for having little faith
and rebuked the winds and the sea, the men marveled,
saying, "What manner of man is this, that even the
winds and sea obey him!" (Matthew 8:27)

Little faith discounts God's power. We may
believe God can do what we've seen Him do. I bet
the disciples had no trouble believing Jesus could
heal the sick and cast out devils because they had
witnessed these displays of Holy Ghost power. But
they marveled when He took authority over the wind
and sea because they hadn't seen Him move that way.
Little faith doesn't believe God can move in ways they
haven't already seen Him move before. That sets up the
believer to get stuck in the midst of a raging storm –
and stuck in the midst of religion. We can't put God
in a box. He is all powerful and He can move any way
He wants. Our job is to ask and believe.

Little Faith is Swayed by Circumstances

You would have thought the disciples would
have learned a thing or two about Jesus in their first

seafaring experience. But just a few chapters later we find the disciples out at sea again. Jesus had instructed them to cross over to the other side – He planned to catch up later. During the fourth watch of the night, Jesus started walking toward them on the sea. When the disciples saw Him, they were terrified and screamed out, "It's a ghost!"

Jesus quickly moved to ease their fears. That's when Peter decided to ask the Lord to bid him to come to Him on the water. Jesus bid him to come. Peter got out of the boat and started walking on the water toward Jesus.

> "But when he saw the wind boisterous, he was afraid; and beginning to sink, he cried, saying, Lord, save me. And immediately Jesus stretched forth his hand, and caught him, and said unto him, O thou of little faith, wherefore didst thou doubt?"(Matthew 14:30-31)

Jesus did ask Peter why He doubted because He didn't know. He knew all along. He knows everything. Jesus asked Peter why he doubted to spur Peter to search his heart for the root of his unbelief and repair that area with faith-filled thoughts and words. Still, you've got to give Peter some credit. He started out with enough faith to walk on water. If Peter had reflected on Jesus' question, he may have discovered that his downfall, or his sinking, as it were, was taking his eyes off Jesus and focusing on the fearful circumstances. Little faith focuses on circumstances instead of the One who can grab your hand and lift you out of those circumstances.

Let's retrace that scene. Peter began to sink. Jesus corrected him, asking why he doubted and told him he had little faith. Peter must have felt pretty silly when the winds stopped so quickly. It was a temporary gust but he was probably expecting a great tempest. Maybe he was thinking about the last time he was out at sea with Jesus and thought He was going to drown. But he should have been thinking about how Jesus rebuked the winds and sea instead. He should have considered the past victories with Christ, not the current state of stormy affairs.

I've had it happen more times than I want to admit. The storm is raging. It looks like I am going to sink, then drown, then wind up at the bottom of the sea for fish food. The pressure gets intense, so intense that you can't figure out how God is going to deliver you from this one. Well, that's part of the problem. God didn't ask us to figure out how He can. He asked us to believe He can.

Lo and behold, each and every time I begin to sink under the pressure, the very next day – sometimes the very next hour – many of the circumstances that were taking my focus off of Jesus subsided. The storm ended. The issues went away. Then I feel pretty stupid. If I had just held out my faith confessions and actions one more day I would have been victorious. Instead,

I failed another test and got to go through it again. It helps to remember that God will never allow more to come on you than you can bear (1 Corinthians 10:3). Actually believing that helps even more.

Little Faith Forgets God's Past Deliverances

In yet another boat ride with Jesus the disciples again demonstrated little faith. Those same disciples had seen Jesus feed the masses on more than one occasion. They had seen Him take loaves and fishes and do a creative miracle out of compassion. How quickly they forgot. Jesus was trying to teach them an important lesson about the doctrines of the Pharisees and Sadducees and all they could think about was the fact that they didn't have any bread on board the ship. Jesus was disappointed that His disciples had so little discernment – and so little faith.

> "Which when Jesus perceived, he said unto them, O ye of little faith, why reason ye among yourselves, because ye have brought no bread? Do ye not yet understand, neither remember the five loaves of the five thousand, and how many baskets ye took up? Neither the seven loaves of the four thousand, and how many baskets ye took up? How

is it that ye do not understand that I spake it not to you concerning bread, that ye should beware of the leaven of the Pharisees and of the Sadducees?" (Matthew 16:8-11)

Jesus must have been especially disappointed considering His earlier sermon about covenant people not worrying about what they would eat or what they would drink. He must have been let down by their reasonings. Human reasoning often leads us into doubt. Reasoning can also block discernment because you'll find an acceptable defense for why something is correct when it's really error, or why something can't be God when it really is.

Little faith forgets the Word of God during times of stress because it's mixed with human reasoning. Little faith forgets God's past deliverances during times of stress. David avoided this by reminding himself of God's faithfulness to deliver him from his enemies. That's one way you transform little faith into great faith.

Chapter 6

MOVING IN MUSTARD SEED FAITH

There was yet one more instance when Jesus had to admonish His disciples for having little faith. You remember the story. Jesus had gone up to a mountain and He was transfigured. It was a glorious scene that surely built faith in Peter, James and John, the trio that witnessed it. While this was happening, some of the disciples were at the bottom of the mountain trying to cast a devil out of a boy. Have you ever seen someone who doesn't understand their authority and only halfway believes in deliverance ministry try to cast a devil out of another person? I have. The devil has a lot of fun with that. The spirits make a real show of it – until someone arrives who has the faith to deal with that devil.

In the case of the boy with devils that threw him into the fire and into the water, that someone was Jesus. When Jesus came down from the mountain, the boy's father greeted Him, and swiftly recounted the scene of the disciples' unsuccessful deliverance meeting. Jesus' reply? He appeared frustrated,

> "O faithless and perverse generation, how long shall I be with you? how long shall I suffer you?" (Matthew 17:17).

Nevertheless, Jesus had compassion on the boy, who was a mere victim, and rebuked the devil. The child was cured. Mission accomplished.

When the dust settled, the disciples wanted to know why they couldn't deal with that devil. If they had listened more closely, they would have already picked up on the problem in Matthew 17:17: it was a matter of faith, or lack thereof, as it were. Then Jesus spoke a parable that was profound. Let's listen in:

> "Then the disciples came to Jesus in private and asked, 'Why couldn't we drive it out?' He replied, 'Because you have so little faith'."
> (Matthew 17:19-20 NIV)

It should be noted that the King James version of this Scripture says exchanges "little faith" for "unbelief." That speaks volumes, doesn't it? You might say it's six of one and half a dozen of the other. A little faith mixed with a little unbelief yields a spiritual goose egg. In other words, the little faith the disciples had wasn't enough to overcome the unbelief in their hearts. God doesn't need you to have mountain-sized faith to work miracles. But he does need pure faith. Let's read on. Jesus told the disciples:

> "I tell you the truth, if you have faith as small as a mustard seed, you can say to this mountain, 'Move from here to there' and it will move. Nothing will be impossible for you'."
> (Matthew 17:20)

Again, you don't need mountain-sized faith to move a mountain. You can do it with faith the size of a grain of mustard seed. Have you ever seen a mustard seed? It's the smallest of all seeds, but Jesus compared it to "a grain of mustard seed, which, when it is sown in the earth, is less than all the seeds that be in the earth: But when it is sown, it groweth up, and becometh greater than all herbs, and shooteth out great branches; so that the fowls of the air may lodge under the shadow of it" (Mark 4:31-32).

The Hindrance of Hybrid Faith

Notice the use of the mustard seed analogy. Jesus uses it in relation to both faith and the Kingdom. We both know it takes faith to operate in the Kingdom. But think about when you first got saved. You didn't have great faith, did you? Faith came to you by hearing someone preach the Word of God. It's likely that you had just enough faith to get you saved. (That's why it's so important for newcomers to Christ to get into a good Bible-based church immediately so they don't backslide into the kingdom of darkness.) But mountain-sized faith is not what got you saved. It was faith the size of a mustard seed that got you saved – but it was pure faith. It wasn't faith mixed with a little unbelief or a little doubt. That wouldn't have gotten the job done.

The same principle holds true for anything you receive from God. Great faith is not necessarily mountain-sized faith. It's pure faith. It's not hybrid faith…Hybrid faith is contaminated faith. A hybrid is something that's mixed, like two animals or two vegetables that have characteristics one of the other put aren't purely either. Maybe you've heard of pluots. It's a mix of a plumb and an apricot. Seedless watermelons are also a hybrid fruit. Interestingly, these fruits won't grow in nature. Indeed, a hybrid is a manipulation of nature.

Bear with me while I draw out this proverb. It's fascinating, really. David Wolfe, a world authority on nutrition who wrote several best-selling books, including "Amazing Grace," has this to say about hybrid fruits and veggies: "They are unnaturally high in sugar and off in the mineral ratios. Hybrid foods are devoid of proper mineral balance that all wild foods contain. So when we eat a lot of hybrid fruit that leads to mineral deficiencies in our bodies. Not only are hybrid fruits and sweet, starchy vegetables unbalanced in minerals, it is eating too much of hybrid sweet fruit and sweet and starchy vegetables that causes the body to bring heavy minerals from the bones into the blood to buffer the hybrid sugar."

Little faith, what I am reckoning as hybrid faith, is much the same. It's high in doubt and off in faith ratios. Hybrid faith is devoid of proper faith balance – which is 100 percent faith. So when we move in hybrid faith, it leads to a deficiency in the ability to receive what we need from God. Do you get the point yet? Mustard seed faith, then, is not hybrid faith. It's pure faith that moves mountains. In what appears to be a sign of the times, Indian researchers have developed a hybrid seed of mustard. Of all things. And guess what they are calling it? Rapeseed-Mustard Seed. An official estimate said there has been a remarkable increase in rapeseed-mustard production and productivity during the last two decades.

Mustard seed faith is great faith. Jesus said this,

> "Verily I say unto you, If ye have faith, and doubt not, ye shall not only do this which is done to the fig tree, but also if ye shall say unto this mountain, Be thou removed, and be thou cast into the sea; it shall be done" (Mathew

21:21). He also said this: "For verily I say unto you, That whosoever shall say unto this mountain, Be thou removed, and be thou cast into the sea; and shall not doubt in his heart, but shall believe that those things which he saith shall come to pass; he shall have whatsoever he saith" (Mark 11:23).

What's your faith saying? Are you speaking pure faith? Out of the abundance of the heart the mouth speaks. Whatever is in your heart in abundance is going to come out when pressure is applied. That's not to say that you have no faith in your heart, but if doubt is coming out of your mouth then the doubt on the particular matter of which you speak is more abundant than the faith on that matter. If it's hybrid faith, it won't have the authority to cast a mountain into the sea or even cast a pebble into a lake, for that matter. But if it's pure faith – great faith that's not defiled by doubt, unbelief and fear – then you shall have whatsoever you say. Every person is given the measure of faith. It comes with the hearing of the Word. It's up to us to purify our heart so that it can grow there unabated.

Chapter 7

GRADUATING TO GREAT FAITH

Now that we understand little faith and mustard seed faith, it's time to examine the type of faith that caused even the Lord Jesus Christ Himself to marvel: great faith. Remember, great faith is mustard seed faith. And mustard seed faith is pure faith. We don't have to wonder what it looks like because the Holy Spirit made record of it in the Bible. Beyond the Old Testament heroes of faith, which we will explore later, it's helpful to look at examples of what Jesus Himself labeled as great faith – and what made it great.

Consider the Canaanite woman from the region of Tyre and Sidon. The Canaanites were old enemies of the Jews, being among the giants in the Promised Land that caused so much fear and doubt to arise in the Israelites. Yet, every knee must bow and every tongue confess that Jesus is Lord, and that's what the Canaanite woman did.

> "Lord, Son of David, have mercy on me! My daughter is suffering terribly from demon-possession (Matthew 15:21-22 NIV).

Jesus ignored her, but apparently, like blind Bartemaeus, she cried out all the more. So much so that Jesus' disciples asked Him to send her away. That's when He responded to the Canaanite woman. Let's listen in on the dialogue that demonstrates great faith in Matthew 15:23-39.

> "I was sent only to the lost sheep of Israel," Jesus insisted.

> The woman came and knelt before him, and replied, "Lord, help me!"

> "It is not right to take the children's bread and toss it to the dogs," Jesus answered.

First, the Canaanite woman had to persist to even get Jesus to take notice of her. Now, she had a chance to get offended with God. He lumped her in the same class as dogs. Given the Apostle Paul's admonition to "beware of dogs," we can discern this was not a kind word. Jesus' response marked a moment of truth for the Canaanite woman. Her daughter was in bondage to a demon spirit. Her only hope was that Jesus, the Deliverer, would show the compassion that she had heard so much about. Her only chance of seeing her daughter set free was the Word of God. So she did what any good mother would do. She was selfless, willing to suffer to put an end to her daughter's suffering. Her response was full of humility, wisdom and grace that got Jesus' attention:

> "Yes, Lord," she said, "but even the dogs eat the crumbs that fall from their masters' table."
>
> Then Jesus answered, "Woman, you have great faith! Your request is granted." And her daughter was healed from that very hour.

Jesus said she had great faith. It was pure faith. She never doubted that He could set her daughter free. Not for a moment. It was persistent faith. She followed Jesus and cried out to Him even when He seemed to ignore her. She wasn't getting any prayer answer. God was silent. But she continued making her request known to God. She kept seeking. She kept knocking. She kept asking. She didn't know it, but she was exercising spiritual laws that were working in her favor all along.

What can we learn from the Canaanite woman? We don't know how many miles she followed Jesus down the road before He noticed her. We don't know how loudly she cried out before He responded. But we do know some things. We know she was persistent. We know that she put her faith in action. We know that she spoke her faith out of her mouth. We know that her request was granted. And we know that Jesus said she had great faith.

A Centurion's Great Faith

The story of the Centurion is familiar. Like the Canaanite woman, he was not part of the Abrahamic covenant. Nevertheless he was able to access the power of God through his faith. The story begins in Matthew 8:5. Jesus enters into Capernaum and is met with a centurion, beseeching him and saying, "Lord, my servant lieth at home sick of the palsy, grievously tormented." Without hesitation, Jesus told the centurion He would come and heal the servant. Like the Canaanite woman, I think Jesus liked the fact that the centurion was interceding on behalf of another. It was selfless faith exercised on behalf of someone who could not help themselves. Jesus likes selflessness. It gets His attention.

Let's listen in on the conversation:

> The centurion told Jesus, "Lord, I am not worthy that thou shouldest come under my roof: but speak the word only, and my servant shall be healed.

For I am a man under authority, having soldiers under me: and I say to this man, Go, and he goeth; and to another, Come, and he cometh; and to my servant, Do this, and he doeth it."

When Jesus heard it, He marveled, and said to them that followed, "Verily I say unto you, I have not found so great faith, no, not in Israel."

And Jesus said unto the centurion, "Go thy way; and as thou hast believed, so be it done unto thee."

The centurion's servant was healed in the selfsame hour. The centurion's petition was granted because he had great faith. What did that look like in practice? Well, again, great faith is pure faith. The centurion never doubted that Jesus could heal his servant. Great faith believes God's Word alone. Great faith understands the authority of the Lord Jesus Christ, and the authority He has given us in His name. Great faith doesn't hesitate to act on what it believes, with the assurance that it shall receive what it is seeking.

The Heroes of Great Faith

Chronicled in the annals of Hebrews 11 you will find many men and women of God who had great faith. We read about Abel and Enoch and Noah.

We learn about Isaac and Jacob and Joseph. But only Abraham is called the father of our faith.

We know that Abram demonstrated great faith when he followed God out of his homeland without even knowing where he was going. That was just the beginning for Abraham. He would fight greater faith battles in his lifetime, among the greatest was obtaining the promise that he would become a father of many nations.

I like how the Amplified version of the Bible brings out Abraham's story in Romans 4:18-21. The Apostle Paul, inspired by the Holy Spirit, told Abraham's story this way:

> [For Abraham, human reason for] hope being gone, hoped in faith that he should become the father of many nations, as he had been promised, So [numberless] shall your descendants be.
>
> He did not weaken in faith when he considered the [utter] impotence of his own body, which was as good as dead because he was about a hundred years old, or [when he considered] the barrenness of Sarah's [deadened] womb.
>
> No unbelief or distrust made him waver (doubtingly question) concerning the promise of God, but

> he grew strong and was empowered
> by faith as he gave praise and glory to
> God, Fully satisfied and assured that
> God was able and mighty to keep His
> word and to do what He had promised.

Abraham had great faith. What does great faith look like? Great faith believes when human reason for hope is gone. Great faith doesn't consider the impotence of our humanity. Great faith remembers the promise of God. Great faith does not make room for unbelief or distrust. Great faith doesn't waver or doubtingly question the promise of God. Great faith strengthens itself for battle by praising and giving glory to God. Great faith focuses on God's ability and God's power to watch over His Word to perform it and make good on His promise. And we know that great faith obtains the promise.

The Great Faith Duo

Joshua and Caleb had great faith. When Moses sent the 12 spies into Canaan to explore the land, 10 came back with an evil report. That's because they had little faith. They saw giants in the land and fear led them into doubt and unbelief. Little faith walks by the five senses and the vain imaginations of the mind. But Joshua and Caleb had a good report – a faith report. They saw God's promises of a land flowing with milk and honey. When Joshua and Caleb saw the giants in the land, the same spirit of fear that was speaking to the minds of the 10 probably spoke to them, too. But instead of agreeing with the grasshopper image fear was reflecting on them, they reflected on God's promise to give them the land. Listen in on the scene. You'll hear the voice of fear, the voice of faith, and the voice of God in The Message translation of Numbers 14:1-15:

> The whole community was in an uproar, wailing all night long. All the People of Israel grumbled against Moses and Aaron. The entire community was in on it: "Why didn't we die in Egypt? Or in this wilderness? Why has God brought us to this country to kill us? Our wives and children are about to become plunder. Why don't we just head back to Egypt? And right now!"
>
> Soon they were all saying it to one another: "Let's pick a new leader; let's head back to Egypt."
>
> Moses and Aaron fell on their faces in front of the entire community, gathered in emergency session.
>
> Joshua son of Nun and Caleb son of Jephunnch, members of the scouting party, ripped their clothes and addressed the assembled People of

Israel: "The land we walked through and scouted out is a very good land—very good indeed. If God is pleased with us, he will lead us into that land, a land that flows, as they say, with milk and honey. And he'll give it to us. Just don't rebel against God! And don't be afraid of those people. Why, we'll have them for lunch! They have no protection and God is on our side. Don't be afraid of them!"

But, up in arms now, the entire community was talking of hurling stones at them.

Just then the bright Glory of God appeared at the Tent of Meeting. Every Israelite saw it. God said to Moses, "How long will these people treat me like dirt? How long refuse to trust me? And with all these signs I've done among them! I've had enough—I'm going to hit them with a plague and kill them. But I'll make you into a nation bigger and stronger than they ever were."

Whoa! God was insulted by the unbelief of the Israelites. So much so that He was ready to do away with the whole faithless crew. If Moses hadn't interceded, the story could have turned out much differently. The point is, God doesn't take kindly to unbelief, especially when He has come through for you time and time again. The Israelites had no excuse not to believe God after all the mighty signs and wonders He performed on their behalf. That shows you the power of the forces of fear, doubt and unbelief. These spirits use reason to bait you, but these spirits are unreasonable because even reason would have lead the Israelites to believe in God's might to deliver on His promises.

What does great faith look like in Joshua and Caleb's story? Great faith is grieved by doubt and unbelief. Great faith says what God says about every situation. Great faith believes God is not a man that He should lie. Great faith knows God is our victory banner and if He calls you to battle you cannot lose. Great faith doesn't fear what it sees with its natural eyes. Great faith inherits the promise.

Even Greater Faith

God taught Abraham how to believe through experience. Abraham's faith grew through each test and trial. But if it took great faith to believe for Isaac, it took perhaps even greater faith to be willing to sacrifice the boy at God's command. I can just imagine the battle against Abraham's mind when God told him to take his son Isaac up to a mountain and slay him.

The Bible says Abraham rose early in the morning to get on his way. Abraham's great faith didn't give the devil a chance to talk him out of it. Oh, I am convinced doubt, unbelief and fear were trying to find a way in as he took that long journey with his only begotten son. By Abraham considered Him.

Abraham's great faith helped him to cast down every imagination and every high and lofty thing that would exalt itself against the knowledge of God (2 Corinthians 10:5). So great was Abraham's faith at this point in his life that when God told him to sacrifice Isaac he accounted that God was able to raise him up, even from the dead. There is no record in the Bible that Abraham had never seen anyone raised from the dead, but He had just that much faith in Jehovah. God could have raised Isaac up, but our loving God didn't make Abraham go that far. Seeing his faith in action through his obedience to go so far as raising the knife was more than enough for God.

The point is this: Once you win victory over doubt and unbelief, your faith will begin growing as you exercise it in Christ. God may ask you to do something that seems impossible, just to see if you'll follow His lead and take faith-filled action toward your destiny. But, many times, you won't have to take that final step. He may lead you right up to the edge of the cliff and then tell you to stop right before you take that final leap of faith. He may test your heart to show you where your faith is. He already knows what's in your heart, but sometimes you need to see it for yourself.

So let's forge ahead to eradicate the doubt and unbelief in our hearts so we can walk in great faith that enables those greater works Jesus spoke of (John 14:12). Who knows, maybe your name will be recorded in the Hall of Faith. God is still keeping record.

Chapter 8

RECOGNIZING THE SYMPTOMS OF DOUBTAHOLISM

D oubt is the doorway to unbelief because the skeptic must first question the Source of information before he is finally unwilling to accept the truth. If doubt is dangerous, then, as we've seen in early chapters, unbelief can be deadly. At the very least it can cripple your prayer life. Ponder this: If it only takes faith the size of a grain if mustard seed to move a mountain, then how much doubt does it take to cancel out a prayer? Selah. Jesus said, "Only believe."

Like any disease, doubtaholism doesn't usually kill your belief all at once. Rather, it manifests in progressive stages. The early symptoms are confusion and inaction. Left unchecked, we move on to fear and anxiety. Finally, we continue to instability, double-mindedness and backtracking that leave us unable to receive the wisdom of God. James, the apostle of practical faith, encourages believers to ask the Lord for direction as needed – in faith, with no wavering, hesitating or doubting.

> "For the one who wavers (hesitates, doubts) is like the billowing surge out at sea that is blown hither and thither and tossed by the wind. For truly, let not such person imagine he will receive anything [he asks for] from the Lord, [For being as he is] a man of two minds (hesitating, dubious, irresolute), [he is] unstable and unreliable and uncertain about everything [he thinks, feels, decides] (James 1:6-8 AMP).

Double-minded and dubious? That may seem like a pretty harsh statement to the doubter, but no worse, I suppose, than God's indictment of the evil heart of unbelief (Hebrews 3:12). What we have to understand is this: God takes doubt and unbelief seriously. Doubting His Word is a blight on His character. Suggesting God won't do what His Word promises is an insult to God, a slap in His holy face. When you understand the heart of God, you'll understand that He has done everything in His power to get you what you need. He gave you His only begotten Son. He gave you His blood. He gave you His name. He gave you His Word. He gave you His Spirit. Now it's up to you – and doubt is enemy number one.

Don't Let Doubt Do Your Decision-Making

Whether you are a full-blown fretting doubtaholic or merely sip from the cup of cautious hesitation, it's important to recognize the symptoms of this spiritual state because it can kill your faith. I'm reminded of the British Heart Foundation "Doubt Kills" campaign that aims to raise awareness of heart attack symptoms and encourage people to take action when they experience them.

A shocking 91 percent of Londoners would not recognize the symptoms of a heart attack, and almost as many would be too embarrassed to call emergency services until chest pains because critical. The people surveyed didn't know that suffering a mild discomfort in the chest that makes you feel generally unwell could be their body warning them.

Doubt attacks the child of God's believing heart. But recognizing the symptoms as early as possible helps us to avoid a life-long debilitation. Don't be too embarrassed to call for emergency prayer. Don't wait until doubt is doing your decision-making for you. Recognize the symptoms of doubt early on and get your help from the Word of God and from faith-filled believers that have overcome in your area of struggle and can help you battle against the weapons of unbelief.

With that said, let's take a closer look at doubt as the doorway to unbelief and its symptoms. It's time we see this sinister spirit for what it is and silence its nagging voice so we can walk in peace, faith – and victory.

Exposing Doubt's Silent Symptoms

Confusion is a symptom of doubt. Think about it for a minute. Confusion is to be perplexed or disconcerted. It also means to be disoriented with regard to your sense of identity. Confusion belongs in the enemy's camp, not in the believer's mind. Confusion is part of the curse of the law (Deuteronomy 28:20). We've been redeemed from the curse of the law, so when confusion presents itself – when we aren't sure what to do now – we know that it's the enemy trying to get us to second guess the will of God.

God's Word prescribes an answer to every problem, a creative solution to every challenge. The Bible is a Book of answers. Confusion doesn't belong to the child of God, and God is not the author of confusion (1 Corinthians 14:33). When we know who we are in Christ and we know the will of the Lord, there is no room for confusion. Confusion, therefore, is an earmark of doubt.

Worry is a sin. Dr. Hagin used to say that worry was a much worse habit than tobacco. Worrying won't grow your stature one cubit but it will absolutely stunt your spiritual growth. Jesus said not to worry about what we're going to eat or what we're going to drink or what we are going to wear (Matthew 6:31). If you are a worrywart (an ugly name for an ugly habit) then try this exercise.

Use Matthew 6:31 as a template and fill in the blank, like this: Therefore, do not worry about (fill in the blank). Jesus doesn't want us to worry about anything at any time. He's got your back. We're instructed to cast all of our cares on Him because He cares for us (1 Peter 5:7). So if you are worrying, if you are burdened down with cares, it's a sure sign that doubt is on the prowl.

Doubt's Red Alerts

Fear and anxiety are red alerts to doubt. Jesus said, "Fear not. Only believe" (Luke 8:50). You can't believe and fear at the same time. It's just not possible. We connect with God through faith, and we connect with Satan through fear.

Satan uses fear as an inroad to steal our faith. So far as anxiety is concerned, even Mirriam-Webster draws the connection between anxiety and doubt: an abnormal and overwhelming sense of apprehension and fear often marked by physiological signs (as sweating, tension, and increased pulse), by doubt concerning the reality and nature of the threat, and by self-doubt about one's capacity to cope with it.

When fear or anxiety comes your way, sound the alarm and go on the offense. There's nothing more important at that moment than getting that fear off you because, again, that's your connection to the devil. You can't fellowship with devilish doubt and God-like faith at the same time. See your enemy and take him out.

Doubt's Not-So Silent Symptoms

Sometimes doubt is not so silent. It comes straight out of our mouths. I can locate my faith by listening to my words because out of the abundance of the heart the mouth speaks (Matthew 12:34). What does that mean? It means whatever is in your heart in abundance is going to come out of your mouth when the pressure is on. Like a teapot on a hot stove, when the contents of that teapot begin to boil over it spews out the spout and makes enough noise to demand your attention.

What's in your teapot? What's in your heart in abundance? Listen to what you speak when everything isn't going your way. Are words of fear coming out of your mouth? Listen carefully and you'll know where to target your efforts in rooting out doubt and planting the word of faith. Begin by saying the opposite of doubt to counter that specific train of thought that seeped out of your holy mouth.

Your actions – or your inactions – can also demonstrate your doubt. The Bible says faith without works is dead (James 2:17). The Amplified translation says faith needs deeds and actions of obedience to back it up because those actions give it power. I also like The Message translation of James 2:17-18:

> "Dear friends, do you think you'll get anywhere in this if you learn all the right words but never do anything? Does merely talking about faith indicate that a person really has it?... Isn't it obvious that God-talk without God-acts is outrageous nonsense? I can already hear one of you agreeing by saying, 'Sounds good. You take care of the faith department, I'll handle the works department.' Not so fast. You can no more show me your works apart from your faith than I can show you my faith apart from my works. Faith and works, works and faith, fit together hand in glove."

You simply cannot demonstrate faith without action. Living faith demands action, not dead works. So if you are paralyzed by the fear, then that means you've let doubt creep in and make your faith inoperative.

Reasoning's Double-Mindedness

Have you ever noticed that doubt likes to reason with you? I love to watch a good debate. The quips, the comebacks, the facts and figures that prove a point. While I like to keep an open mind, in the end I always side with one speaker or another on any given issue. God has given us the ability to reason, to exercise our mind, to draw conclusions based on facts. It's when we rely on logic rather than God's Word that reasoning leads us into confusion, doubt and ultimately unbelief.

Think about it for a minute. Have you ever tried to reason something out with a friend and left the conversation more confused than you were when you sought the advice? When you stumble into confusion, your reasoning has gone to far. You need to back up and find out what the Word of God says – and then believe it. To do anything else is to run the risk of instability and double-mindedness, two more symptoms of doubt.

Remember this: When you ask God "how?" that's a doubtful disputation. Listen, no condemnation. Even great men and women in the Bible doubted from time to time. Remember John the Baptist? He prophesied the coming of the Lord and baptized Him in the Jordan River, but when pressure clouded his head, he asked, "Are you the Messiah or should we look for another?" (Matthew 11:2). Doubtless, the spirit of doubt was whispering to John the same way it whispers to us – questioning if the Lord is Who He says He is in our lives.

Armed with an understanding of these symptoms, you can begin to ward off doubt's evil. In the next chapter, we'll look at the dream-killer called self-doubt and how it seeks not only to kill your prayer life but also destroy your destiny.

Chapter 9

SELF-DOUBT: THE DREAM KILLER

D oubting God's Word can lead to another paralyzer: self-doubt. If you doubt what God's Word says about you, either His written Word or His tried and proven-authentic prophetic Word, then you won't dare to dream. Self-doubt is what I call a dream killer. It releases the wrong kinds of imaginations.

God gave us an imagination. It's part of our soulish realm. Imagination is the act or power of forming a mental image of something not present to the senses or never before wholly perceived in reality. It could also be defined as creative ability.

Where would the great literary masterpieces from Shakespeare, Mark Twain and Ernest Hemingway be without imagination? Non-existent. Where would classic thrillers from Alfred Hitchcock and Steven Spielberg be without imagination? Again, non-existent. Where would airplanes and cars and many of the innovations we enjoy today be without imagination? Nowhere to be found. Could it be possible that man would be stuck in the Dark Ages without imagination; without man's willingness to dream of a better way and believe that those dreams can come true?

Consider Thomas Edison. He tried to invent the light bulb hundreds of times before he met with success. What if he had given up on his dream; abandoned his imagination? What if he had doubted himself? Helen Keller (1880-1968) proved that you don't need the ability to see with your natural eyes in order to dream a seemingly impossible dream.

Keller was an American author and educator who was both blind and deaf. She was the first deaf and blind person to graduate from college. (Pick up the book The Miracle Worker if you want to read her incredible, inspiring story.) Keller campaigned for women's suffrage, worker's rights and was an outspoken opponent of war. Here's what she had to say about doubt:

> "Doubts and mistrust are the mere panic of timid imagination, which the steadfast heart will conquer, and the large mind transcend."

Self-Doubt: A Traitor Cloaked in Fear

I also like what Shakespeare said, "Our doubts are traitors and make us lose the good we oft might win, by fearing to attempt." It's simply impossible to fight the good fight of faith while doubting at the same time. For some of you, you may need to fight against your own insecurities that try to convince you that you everyone else can see the Word work in their lives but you; that everyone else can see dreams come true but you. You've got to fight doubt like a devil, because that's what it is.

For me, I've struggled with doubting God's grace in time-sensitive situations more than once. We know that God is always on time, He's never late, but He's rarely early – or so it's been said. You might describe me the same way. I have a lot of deadlines – daily deadlines, actually, multiple deadlines daily – and when the heat is really on the temptation is to doubt I can meet those deadlines because naturally speaking there's no way I could do it.

Compounding the issue is the fact that I am a recovering perfectionist (though I prefer to characterize myself as 'in pursuit of a spirit of excellence'). That means not only do tasks have to be completed quickly, they need to be right on target. I have to resist the overwhelm that comes with whispering doubts telling me it will never get done, and giving me imaginations about the repercussions of missing the deadlines. What I learned was that focusing on what might not get done caused me to want to give up and not even try.

For some people, doubt's magnifying glass on what might not happen can cause them to decide not to try before they even start. Two-time Olympian figure skating medalist Nancy Kerrigan put it this way: "Doubt yourself and you doubt everything you see. Judge yourself and you see judges everywhere. But if you listen to the sound of your own voice, you can rise above doubt and judgment. And you can see forever." In our case, we need to listen to the sound of God's voice. He says we can do all things through Christ who strengthens us (Philippians 4:13).

Self-Doubt Angers God

If you see self-doubt in your heart, don't get under condemnation. You aren't the only one. Some great men of God struggled to believe they could be everything God called them to be.

Moses was a great prophet of God, but God had to deliver Moses from doubt before Moses could deliver Israel from Egypt. You know the story. Moses saw a burning bush and stopped to see the sight. God spoke to him about His plans to bring Israel out of bondage and told Moses step one was confronting Pharaoh. Moses' response? Who am I, that I should go unto Pharaoh, and that I should bring forth the children of Israel out of Egypt? (Exodus 3:11).

God tried to reassure Moses that He'd be with him, then explained the next steps: "Go tell Israel the game plan. Tell the children of the covenant they will soon be free from Pharaoh's grip. Then go tell Pharaoh I said to let you travel into the wilderness and worship me. Pharaoh won't let you go right away, but in the end you'll leave with the spoils." Moses' response? "They won't believe me or do what I say. They'll think I'm making this up!" I can understand Moses' hesitation here. I mean…that's a pretty wild story in some sense. But Moses doubted his own credibility with the people. He didn't doubt God. He doubted himself.

Well, God helped Moses through that personal identity crisis, only to find Moses with another self-doubting excuse:

> "And Moses said unto the Lord, O my Lord, I am not eloquent, neither heretofore, nor since thou hast spoken unto thy servant: but I am slow of speech, and of a slow tongue" (Exodus 3:10).

God reassured Moses once again that He would be with him. Moses still objected and God's patience was finally exhausted. The Bible says "the anger of the Lord was kindled against Moses." He told Moses that Aaron would speak for him as he spoke for God. But that wasn't God's original intention. Moses' self-doubt forced God to find a creative solution to getting His will done in the earth.

The Doubting Duo

Jeremiah also battled self-doubt. The word of the Lord came to him saying, "Before I formed thee in the belly I knew thee; and before thou camest forth out of the womb I sanctified thee, and I ordained thee a prophet unto the nations" (Jeremiah 1:5). What an awesome prophetic word! You would think Jeremiah would have been excited, awestricken or at least curious. But his immediate reaction revealed the self-doubt in his heart: "I can't speak. I'm just a kid!" God told young Jerry not to worry about his age and went on to commission him. Jeremiah didn't throw up excuses the way Moses did. Maybe he learned a thing or two from reading the ancient scrolls.

Remember Gideon? God called him to be a deliverer and the first words out of his mouth were:

"Me, my master? How and with what could I ever save Israel? Look at me. My clan's the weakest in Manasseh and I'm the runt of the litter" (Judges 6:15 The Message). God's response? "I'll be with you. Believe me, and you won't be defeated."

Therein lies the answer to self-doubt: believe God. God doesn't like self-doubt because self-doubt ultimately or eventually also doubts God. God told Moses He would be with him, but Moses' own self-doubt was so great that he couldn't even believe God.

Gideon's self-doubt was so great that he asked God to give him a sign before he was satisfied. If God has called you to do something, whether that's tackle a new project in the marketplace or launch a new ministry, don't look at who you aren't. Look at who He is. Don't doubt yourself. American author and editor Christian N. Bovee once offered these wise words: "Doubt whom you will, but never yourself." Believe God because he believes in you. He will never leave you or forsake you.

Self-doubt is a dream killer. God-trust is a lifeline that infuses you with power to walk out your dreams in Him.

Chapter 10

ADMIT, CONFESS, REPENT AND BELIEVE THE GOSPEL

D oubtless, you've heard of 12-step programs. Founded in 1935 by Bill Wilson and Dr. Bob Smith, Alcoholics Anonymous was the first known 12-step program in the world. Today, there are 12-step programs to help people break all kinds of addictions, and these programs have found great success in millions of cases. While our endeavor is not to mimic the famed 12 steps, per se, I have developed Bible-based steps for breaking free from doubt and unbelief. So if you are ready to get free from doubtaholism, let's get started on the journey that guarantees victory.

Step 1: Admit You Have Problem

The first step to recovering from doubtaholism is to see this debilitating disease for what it really is: sin. The Bible says whatever is not of faith is sin (Romans 14:23). The Bible also says without faith it is impossible to please God (Hebrews 11:6).

If you want to get free from doubtaholism, whether it's an occasional drink or a chronic illness, you need to recognize you have a problem and then admit it. Admit that it's a sin. You aren't alone. We all have doubts from time to time. Admitting the issue puts you on the path to deliverance. Denying it opens the door for doubt to lead you into full-blown unbelief. The Apostle John put it this way:

> "If we say we have no sin [refusing to admit that we are sinners], we delude and lead ourselves astray, and the Truth [which the Gospel presents] is not in us [does not dwell in our hearts]. 1 John 1:7-9 (Amplified)

Don't make excuses about how your grandma doubted, your mama doubted, and you have doubt ingrained on your heart. Don't let pride, shame or anything else stand in the way of you getting free! Yes, doubtaholism is a serious issue, but God's arm is not too short to reach down and help us out of this unbelieving pit. We have to humble ourselves under

His mighty hand and admit to ourselves we haven't been walking in faith.

This is your first step toward true faith in Christ. Nineteenth century clergyman Theodore Ledyard Cuyler said this: "Every step toward Christ kills a doubt. Every thought, word, and deed for Him carries you away from discouragement." I like that. When we are in doubt, we are no doubt discouraged. There is no peace where there is doubt. There is no joy where there is doubt. There is no boldness where there is doubt. There are no prayer answers where there is doubt.

Step 2: Confess Your Fault

Once you've admitted to yourself that you have a doubt problem, the next step is telling others. Indeed, healing begins with confessing the fault. The Bible says, "Confess to one another therefore your faults (your slips, your false steps, your offenses, your sins) and pray [also] for one another, that you may be healed and restored [to a spiritual tone of mind and heart]" (James 5:16 AMP). The prayer of a person living right with God is something powerful to be reckoned with. Repent to god for your doubt and unbelief.

Repentance is a wonderful privilege. Think about it for a minute: the devil can't repent. Only believers can repent. So if you've decided to repent, you are well on your way to victory because it shows your faith in

God's willingness to forgive. So many Christians are drowning in the sea of condemnation instead of letting God throw their sin into the sea of forgetfulness.

God wants us to be sorrowful over our sin. But He doesn't want us to stay sorrowful. Take a few minutes to really reflect on how your doubt and unbelief hurt God, truly see your doubtaholism as something that came against God's integrity, His character, His honor. Don't merely be sorry that you've been missing out on God's promises. Be sorry that you've restricted God's plans and purposes in the earth with your doubt and unbelief. It's really not about us. It's about Him working through us to reach the world. Our doubt and unbelief hinders His plan. See it for what it is – and now get ready to let it go.

Step 3: Receive God's Forgiveness

Now repent – and take a moment to receive His forgiveness. Say, "God, I thank you for your forgiveness and I receive it right now by faith, in Jesus' name." That is pleasing to God. Congratulations. You are ready to begin walking by faith again. Consider what God's Word has to say about repentance and forgiveness and be encouraged.

Let's remind ourselves of 1 John 1:9, the condemnation-buster that drives the devil mad.

"If we confess our sins, he is faithful and just to forgive us our sins, and to cleanse us from all unrighteousness."

Read it again in the Amplified version:

"If we [freely] admit that we have sinned and confess our sins, He is faithful and just (true to His own nature and promises) and will forgive our sins [dismiss our lawlessness] and [continuously] cleanse us from all unrighteousness [everything not in conformity to His will in purpose, thought, and action]."

And The Message Bible to drill it home in plain language.

"On the other hand, if we admit our sins—make a clean breast of them—he won't let us down; he'll be true to himself. He'll forgive our sins and purge us of all wrongdoing."

Don't get into works of the flesh trying to make it up to God. Our righteousness is like filthy rags (Isaiah 64:4-9). Failing to receive the blood of Jesus as the only worthy – and the only required – payment for your sin is an insult to God. Is the blood of Jesus not sufficient to wash away our sins? Of course, it is. Once you've repented and asked for forgiveness, there is no need for guilt trips, condemnation corners or works-based penance. You are free in Christ. Don't doubt it.

Now, here comes the real deliverance. After you've admitted you have a problem, confessed your faults and repented before God, it's time to move in the opposite spirit: faith. You relied on God to forgive you, now start relying on God in other areas of your life.

Chapter 11

GETTING TO THE HEART OF THE MATTER

N ow we're going to get to the heart of the matter: your heart. The Bible says out of the abundance of the heart the mouth speaks (Matthew 12:34). That means whatever is in your heart in abundance is going to eventually come out of your mouth. Sure, you may sound super-spiritual in church, but what happens when the pressure comes in the marketplace? Will you continue speaking words of faith or will doubt ooze from between your should-be sanctified lips?

Steps four and five in our 12-step process deal with the heart. Consider how David prayed to the Lord. He asked God to examine him, and prove him, and try the reigns of his heart (Psalm 26:2). The Message translation reads this way:

> "Examine me, God, from head to foot, order your battery of tests. Make sure I'm fit inside and out." The psalmist also prayed, "Investigate my life, O God, find out everything about me; Cross-examine and test me, get a clear picture of what I'm about; See for yourself whether I've done anything wrong— then guide me on the road to eternal life (Psalm 139:23 The Message).

Some would be afraid to pray that way because they doubt they would pass the battery of tests. But that's the point exactly...God already knows what's in your heart. If you've got doubt in there, He knows it. But you can't rid yourself of it until you know it. Of course, there is no once-and-for-all in the realm of doubt and unbelief. Once you get rid of these bad roots, you have to take the advice of David's son Solomon:

> "Keep thy heart with all diligence; for out of it are the issues of life" (Proverbs 4:23).

With this preface, let's look at steps four and five.

Step 4: Examine Your Heart

When you truly repent, then your effective, fervent prayers will bear fruit. Of course, doubt will try to enter your heart again. Don't doubt the devil's craftiness. This devil will lie in wait until a strategic moment when you appear to be vulnerable, and then begin whispering again to lead you back into doubtaholism. If he can get you to entertain one little doubt – take one little drink – then he's got you back on the wrong path. That's why after you repent you need to immediately search your heart to determine what allowed the doubt and unbelief to enter in the first place. I like the way the Apostle Paul put it to the church at Corinth:

> "Test yourselves to make sure you are solid in the faith. Don't drift along taking everything for granted. Give yourselves regular checkups. You need firsthand evidence, not mere hearsay, that Jesus Christ is in you. Test it out. If you fail the test, do something about it. I hope the test won't show that we have failed. But if it comes to that, we'd rather the test showed our failure than yours. We're rooting for the truth to win out in you. We couldn't possibly do otherwise)."
> (2 Corinthians 13:5 The Message)

In other words, know that you know that you know that you are on faith-filled footing. You don't want to end up back in the grips of doubtaholism, and maybe even worse than you were. Is it the environment you grew up in that steeped you in doubt? While that's no excuse, it may be a reason to be extra cautious in your old stomping grounds. Has a life filled with disappointment caused you to be a doubter? Get reappointed. Christ in you is the hope. Are you still trying to win the battle in your mind that's been raging for decades? Get the reinforcements you need to finally break free from those bondages.

The point is to close any doors through which doubt might sneak. As a matter of fact, don't just close them – slam them shut with righteous indignation. Writer Edith Armstrong once said, "I keep the telephone of my mind open to peace, harmony, health, love and abundance. Then whenever doubt, anxiety, or fear try to call me, they keep getting a busy signal and soon they'll forget my number."

Like Saul, when we turn toward God in obedience, He can give us another heart (1 Samuel 10:9). God has already made you a new creature in Christ Jesus, but if you are still holding on to some of your old ways – doubt, cynicism, whatever you want to call it – then ask God to give you a new heart. David was a man after God's own heart (Acts 13:22). The Bible says his heart was perfect toward God (1 Kings 11:4). It wasn't because he never made a mistake. It was because he always trusted in the Lord and repented when he misstepped.

Step 5: Guard Your Heart

Now that you can see clearly how you got into the dire straights of doubt – and now that God has pulled you from the quick sand of skepticism, you are well on your way to recovering from doubtaholism. But, like an alcoholic, you'll need to show fruits of repentance. That means quit taking shots of doubt. Don't even blend a doubt-faith mixer. No doubt on the rocks. Build your faith on the Rock instead.

In the Book of Deuteronomy, God commands us to:

1. Love the Lord our God with all our heart and soul and;

2. To turn to Him with all our heart and;

3. To obey Him with all our heart and all our soul.

We can't love, trust and obey Him in areas where doubt and unbelief has taken up residence in our hearts and souls. Don't let the strange god of doubt drive back into your heart.

If sifting the doubt out of your faith means avoiding certain family members or friends until your faith is pure enough to combat the doubtful disputations they offer, then avoid them and hang out with some faith-filled warriors instead. Like Zebulun, faith-filled warriors are expert in battle, with all instruments of war, they can keep rank and they are not of double heart (1 Chronicles 12:33).

What am I saying? I'm telling you to guard your heart. In fact, you'll need to circumcise the foreskin of your hearts. Unbelief causes a callous to form that must be cut away in order for us to believe wholeheartedly (Deuteronomy 10:16).

The situation you find yourself in is not unlike getting diagnosed with high cholesterol. It hardens your arteries and can lead to coronary heart disease if you don't catch it soon enough. Once you receive the diagnoses, you sometimes have to make significant changes to your diet in order to cleanse your arteries. When it comes to spiritual hardening, the same holds true. Instead of feeding on doubt and unbelief, you need to feed on the Word of faith. Just as your cardiologist would tell you to eliminate foods high in saturated fat from your diet, the Great Cardiologist warns us to eliminate thoughts that are high in saturated doubt from our spiritual diets.

So do what King Solomon said in Proverbs 4:23. The Message Bible puts it this way:

> "Keep vigilant watch over your heart;
> that's where life starts. Don't talk out

of both sides of your mouth; avoid careless banter, white lies, and gossip. Keep your eyes straight ahead; ignore all sideshow distractions. Watch your step, and the road will stretch out smooth before you. Look neither right nor left; leave evil in the dust."

Chapter 12

TRUST, RENEW, PRAY AND DO

Congratulations. You've admitted you have a problem, confessed your fault, repented and received forgiveness. You have a fresh start, a clean slate, a new beginning. What are you going to do with it? The enemy already knows where you are vulnerable – in your mind. He knows what types of thoughts you are prone to accept and meditate on. He understands your patterns and what it takes to push your buttons. If you want to walk in victory over doubt and all its cohorts, then you need to equip yourself with the truth to combat the devil's lies. Specifically, you need to decide to trust the Lord, renew your mind, pray in the Spirit and be a doer of the Word.

Step 6: Decide to Trust in the Lord

You've come to the point of decision. It's time to make a quality decision to trust the Lord. Notice I said a 'quality' decision. A quality decision comes only after examining the alternatives and the consequences. American General Omar Nelson Bradley once said, "We are given one life, and the decision is ours whether to wait for circumstances to make up our mind, or whether to act, and in acting, to live." Christ is our life, and when we trust in Him we truly live.

True repentance will bring lasting change only when you decide once and for all to trust in the Lord with all your heart instead of trying to figure everything out on your own (Proverbs 3:5). When we try to reason things out in our finite minds, we open the door to doubt because often times we just can't see how God could possibly make good on His Word in our unique situation.

Some of us have a tendency to try to figure things out for God and suggest His course of action instead of praying based on the Scriptures and believing He'll watch over His Word to perform it. Trying to figure it all out is not trusting in the Lord. We are supposed to walk by faith and not by sight – and not by mental reasoning, either (2 Corinthians 5:7). The Lord knows the way. In fact, the Lord is the Way. Make a decision, once and for all, to trust in Him. He will direct your paths. He'll never leave you in the lurch. He is faithful.

Meditate on these Scriptures to help renew your mind to the Lord's trustworthiness and the promised results of believing God.

> The Lord is my strength and my shield; my heart trusted in him, and I am helped: therefore my heart greatly rejoiceth; and with my song will I praise him (Psalm 28:7).

> For our heart shall rejoice in him, because we have trusted in his holy name (Psalm 33:21).

> Trust in him at all times; ye people, pour out your heart before him: God is a refuge for us. Selah (Psalm 62:8).

> Trust in the Lord with all thine heart; and lean not unto thine own understanding. In all your ways acknowledge him and he will direct your paths (Proverbs 3:5).

Do you trust the Lord? I'm sure your answer is yes. Do you doubt His power, His ability, His willingness? I'm sure your answer is no. But worry belies us. We can't worry, which is a step or two past doubt, and trust God at the same time. So when you begin to worry about any little thing, take that as a sign you are not fully trusting God. Some people can trust Him with their finances, but not their family. Some people can trust Him with their health but not their home front. Trusting God is not a selective process. You don't have to worry that He'll let you down. Trust is part of God's character. You can't separate God from trustworthiness anymore than you can separate Him from love and truth.

Again, you have to make a quality decision. Remember, a quality decision looks at the alternatives and the consequences. For Kingdom people, the alternative to not trusting God brings consequences that can hinder our destiny. Get your mind off the immediate circumstances around you and get an eternal perspective on your decisions – then decide to trust the Lord. Keep in mind there's a difference between faith and trust. Faith is believing God's ability to perform His Word. Trust is believing He will come through on time – and He will.

Step 7: Renew Your Mind

Now that you've made a quality decision, it's time to back it up with the Word of God. We began doing this in Step 5 with the Scripture exercise. But I want to reemphasize through the Word how important it is at this stage in your recovery from doubtaholism. Lasting victory depends on renewing your mind with Scriptures about trust in the Lord and reading passages that demonstrate God's faithfulness to His servants over the ages. Go to the eleventh chapter of Hebrews and read about the heroes of faith. See how God rewarded the faith of Abel, Enoch, Noah, Abraham, Sara, Isaac, Jacob, Moses and Rahab.

The writer of Hebrews ran out of time to tell the stories of "Gideon, Barak, Samson, Jephthah, of David and Samuel and the prophets, who by [the help of] faith subdued kingdoms, administered justice, obtained promised blessings, closed the mouths of lions, extinguished the power of raging fire, escaped the devourings of the sword, out of frailty and weakness won strength and became stalwart, even mighty and resistless in battle, routing alien hosts" (Hebrews 11: 32-34 AMP).

I'd say God has a pretty good track record for rewarding those who stand in faith, wouldn't you? God is no respecter of persons. What He did for these men and women of God, He'll do for you – if you don't doubt. Let's review some Scriptures that show the benefits of meditating on God's Word.

> The law of his God is in his heart; none of his steps shall slide (Psalm 37:31).

> My son, attend to my words; incline thine ear unto my sayings. Let them not depart from thine eyes; keep them in the midst of thine heart. For they are life unto those that find them, and health to all their flesh (Proverbs 4:20-23).

Keep my commandments, and live; and my law as the apple of thine eye. Bind them upon thy fingers, write them upon the table of thine heart (Proverbs 7:2-4).

Place these words on your hearts. Get them deep inside you. Tie them on your hands and foreheads as a reminder. Teach them to your children. Talk about them wherever you are, sitting at home or walking in the street; talk about them from the time you get up in the morning until you fall into bed at night. Inscribe them on the doorposts and gates of your cities so that you'll live a long time, and your children with you, on the soil that God promised to give your ancestors for as long as there is a sky over the Earth. Deuteronomy 11:18-21 (The Message)

Don't just read your Bible. Speak the Scriptures out of your mouth day and night. Then you will have good success (Joshua 1:8). Meditating on the Word of God will build your faith. Meditating isn't just for the Bhuddists or the New Agers. God started the idea.

I love Noah Webster's 1828 Dictionary. Its definitions often offer Scripture. It's worth a look at Webster's classic definition of meditate. It means "to think on; to revolve in the mind." Webster offers Psalm 1 as an example, "His delight is in the law of the Lord, and in His law doth he meditate day and night." In Joshua 1:8, the Hebrew word for meditate ("haw-Gaw') gives us another level of meaning: to murmur, ponder, imagine, mutter, speak, study, talk and utter. I submit to you that if we murmur, ponder, imagine, speak, and study the Word of God, our faith will act as a shield to block doubt from our minds. (For those of you who are doubting the suggestion, what do you have to lose?)

I can't stress enough how important it is to meditate on the Word of God. Along with praying in tongues, it is vital to your spiritual growth and maturity because you can agree with the Word all day long but you won't see change in your life until you renew your mind to the truth you say you believe. When your mind is renewed to the Word in any area, it becomes natural for you to walk in the light that you have. It becomes easier to be a doer of the Word than to walk after the ways of the world.

> Let Psalm 19:14 be your prayer: "Let the words of my mouth, and the meditation of my heart, be acceptable in thy sight, O Lord, my strength, and my redeemer."

Step 8: Pray in the Spirit

You can also build yourself up in your most holy faith – and in doing so combat doubt – by praying in tongues. Allowing the Holy Ghost to pray through you will edify your spirit and ensure perfect prayers are being released on your behalf (Jude 1:20). When doubt hits my mind, or when I don't know what to do, I pray in tongues. After all, the Bible says we don't know how to pray as we ought (Romans 8:26). When my spirit is edified, it's so much easier to catch those doubtful imaginations before they have time to take root.

Remember, the parable of the Sower? (Mark 4:1-20). The Sower who sowed the Word was Jesus, but I believe the devil is also sowing words; words of doubt and unbelief and fear and insecurity. Praying in tongues will help us to keep our spirits receptive to the things of God, and, in doing so, guard our hearts and minds in Christ Jesus. Think of praying in tongues as making your shield of faith even stronger, wider, taller than it already is. If you aren't baptized in the Holy Spirit, pray and ask God to fill you to overflowing. Jesus is the Baptizer and He will respond to your hunger and thirst to be filled with the Holy Spirit who will lead and guide you into truth instead of doubt.

What's more, the Apostle Paul offered some awesome insight to the church at Corinth:

> "For he that speaketh in an unknown tongue speaketh not unto men, but

unto God: for no man understandeth
him; howbeit in the spirit he speaketh
mysteries" (1 Corinthians 14:2).

I said earlier that the decisions you make will help
shape your destiny. So will praying in tongues. Praying
in tongues opens up your spirit to more revelation
from the Lord so that we can walk on His path with
a knowing the devil can't take away.

Step 9: Be a Doer of the Word

When we hear the Word and do it, it brings
stability to our lives. Jesus said whoever hears His
sayings and does them is a wise man (Matthew 7:24).
See, doubt is really a form of deception. Doubt is
the devil's way of introducing thoughts, ideas and
suggestions that God's Word isn't worth the ink to
print the book, at least not in your life. You may believe
God's Word works for everybody else, but not for you.
You may even have evidence of the fact. But could it
be possible that you aren't doing the Word in the area
in which you are doubting?

In other words, could it be possible that your
financial struggles are rooted in failing to do the Word
in the area of giving? Or, is it possible that your health
woes are rooted in failing to do Word in the area of
caring for your body? (The Bible suggests rest for our
bodies and activities to avoid. What's more, stress is
a silent killer that causes a myriad of health problems

– and stressing isn't believing or trusting God.) It is entirely possible that your doubt has left you deceived in a given area. You could be blinded to the truth as you grapple for reasons why the Word doesn't work. You may even be blaming God. Reasoning can block your ability to discern God's wisdom about how to get out of your mess. I like the Amplified version of this Scripture because it really sheds light on the matter:

> "But be doers of the Word [obey the message], and not merely listeners to it, betraying yourselves [into deception by reasoning contrary to the Truth]. For if anyone only listens to the Word without obeying it and being a doer of it, he is like a man who looks carefully at his [own] natural face in a mirror; For he thoughtfully observes himself, and then goes off and promptly forgets what he was like. But he who looks carefully into the faultless law, the [law] of liberty, and is faithful to it and perseveres in looking into it, being not a heedless listener who forgets but an active doer [who obeys], he shall be blessed in his doing (his life of obedience). (James 1:22-25, AMP)

Doubt can deceive us when we hear the Word

and say, "I know, I know" even though we aren't really doing it. Doubt can deceive us when we begin reasoning contrary to the Truth. Doubt can deceive us, my friends, when we don't walk in the Word we know. That deception leads to bondage because bondage is merely believing the lies of the enemy. When we walk out the Word by faith, and refuse to doubt, we will be blessed, free, and on our way to receiving God's best.

Chapter 13

FIGHT THE
GOOD FIGHT

The Apostle Paul told Timothy to fight the good fight of faith (1 Timothy 6:12). One day as I was sitting on my balcony overlooking the waterway and studying the Word of God, I ran upon that Scripture. I began to ask the Lord what that meant. What does it really mean to fight the good fight of faith?

Really, I was more concerned with why Paul referred to it as a "good" fight. I've heard it said it's a good fight because we always win. I'm not negating that, but it's good to find out from God for yourself instead of just repeating what's been taught in the Church for decades. When a Scriptures jumps out at you, meditate on it. It could be that the Lord is trying to reveal something to you that will help you and others.

So why is it a good fight? Here's what the Lord showed me: When we fight the good fight of faith we are enforcing His Word, we are taking a stand on God's character, and we are defending His good name. You've probably seen kids arguing on the playground. It sounds something like this:

"My daddy said Alaska used to be part of Russia," says Johnny.

"Nuh-uh," Susie says. "My daddy says it was part of Iceland."

"Nuh-uh. Alaska!"

"No, you dummy. It came from Iceland.

Clearly, both Johnny's father and Susie's father can't both be right. Clearly, one of them is completely wrong. Susie is deceived because she believed something that was not true. This is what the devil does to us. We insist, "My Father says I'm healed, prosperous, and joyful." And Satan's little demons whisper to us, "Nuh-uh, my father says your sick, poor and pitiful." Well, Satan is the father of lies, the father of poverty, the father of sickness, the father of evil. Of course that's what his demons are going to say.

You might have to debate with the devil – you might have to fight the good fight and wrestle against principalities and powers and rulers of darkness and spirits of wickedness in heavenly places – but if you fight the good fight you will indeed win every time. But you have to keep the purpose in perspective. It's not about you. It's about defending God's honor.

Defending God's Honor

When we fight for God, He'll fight for us. The battle really is the Lord's but we are soldiers in His army and we fight for and with Him. A man is only as good as his Word and the same holds true for God. God is not a man that He should lie (Numbers 23:19). We need to get mad with the devil when he dares to bring circumstances or conditions that attempt to defy God's Word.

Again, when the devil attacks us, it's not really about us. It's about hindering and thwarting the plans of God. We need to get our focus off ourselves and on to God's purposes. Can I get painfully real with you? We need to stop feeling sorry for ourselves when the devil attacks us.

Self-pity will keep you from fighting the good fight of faith. Crying and licking your wounds and rehearsing your defeat to friends, family and anyone who will listen leaves the door wide open for another attack. When we get focused on ourselves instead of God and His Word, the devil can side swipe us.

Stop feeling sorry for yourself because you haven't seen your healing manifest. Stop feeling sorry for yourself because you don't have as much money as Sister So and So. Stop feeling sorry for yourself and start defending God's honor. Is He not worthy of all the honor and glory and dominion? You defend God's honor through your expressed faith and your active faith – nothing wavering. When we do, we'll fight the good fight of faith and win every time. So let's learn how to fight the good fight in Step 10.

Step 10: Fight the Good Fight

Since the battle is in the mind, keeping yourself from returning to the cup of doubt will require you to fight the good fight of faith (1 Timothy 6:12). Faith speaks what the Word says even when circumstances defy it. Remember Abraham? He didn't deny his circumstances, but he did defy his circumstances by his faith.

> "Against all hope, Abraham in hope believed and so became the father of many nations, just as it had been said to him, 'So shall your offspring be.' Without weakening in his faith, he faced the fact that his body was as

good as dead—since he was about a hundred years old—and that Sarah's womb was also dead. Yet he did not waver through unbelief regarding the promise of God, but was strengthened in his faith and gave glory to God, being fully persuaded that God had power to do what he had promised."
Romans   4:18-21(NIV)

I love it! Abraham faced the facts, but then he used his faith to defy them! He didn't doubt God, or His power to bring life to their "good as dead" bodies. He didn't doubt that God would watch over His prophetic word to perform it. He didn't doubt it for a nanosecond. Instead, he gave glory to God – and that strengthened his faith. I like this because some folk who claim to be walking by faith completely deny the existence of a thing. They could be sneezing, sniffling, coughing, aching, and stuffy headed, with a fever and need some rest. But instead of praying and taking a good dose of Nyquil, you'll ask them how they are and they'll say, "I am perfectly fine." If you insinuate they might have a cold, they get offended! But that's not real faith. Faith doesn't deny the existence of the circumstance. Faith uses words to bring those circumstances back in line with God's will. It calls those thing that be not as though they were until they be.

Fighting the good fight also entails doing your

part. You could put it like this: "Faith without works is dead" (James 2:17). Or, you might say it this way: "So also faith, if it does not have works (deeds and actions of obedience to back it up), by itself is destitute of power (inoperative, dead) (James 2:17 AMP).

Listen, the demons don't doubt God or His power. When doubt comes against you, exercise your faith with an action. Sometimes that's as simple as opening your mouth and speaking the Word to slice the enemy's thoughts, ideas and suggestions to smithereens. Sometimes that means applying for that well-paying job that no one, especially you, thinks you can get – but God told you to seek. In my case, fighting the good fight of faith meant moving into a condo before we inked the deal.

Fighting for the Promised Condo

It was the summertime and the apartment I was renting was being converted to a condo for sale. They made us all move out and find new places to live during the renovation – and we had no opportunity to come back. Instead of renting another pad, I decided to purchase my own condo on the beach. All well and good, but I had some credit issues that made it impossible to qualify for a loan. Even though the issues were largely bogus and were later removed, my hands were tied by the Canaanite system. Hoping against hope, I moved forward to purchase a condo anyway. The mortgage broker assured me he could pull off the deal and the paperwork would be in place when I returned from my mission trip to Nicaragua. During my quiet time there, I was talking to the Lord about it and He gave me a Scripture: Jeremiah 32:10.

Well, I don't mind admitting that wasn't a Scripture I had memorized, but I will never forget it again. Jeremiah 32:10 says this:

> "And I signed the deed and sealed it, called witnesses, and weighed out for him the money on the scales" (AMP).

Wow! That verse really edified me because I was concerned about the devil attempting to steal, kill and destroy the deal while I was out on the harvest field reaping. But as I meditated on that Scripture I was filled to overflowing with confidence and began repeating what the Lord told me to anyone who would listen. I was excited about going home and moving into my new condo. But when I returned to Miami I was greeted with some unexpected news: the deal was delayed.

So confident was I that I convinced the seller's agent to let me go ahead and move into the condo. I couldn't stay at my apartment because they forced us all out. And I didn't want to store all of my belongings in a facility, stay at a hotel, and then move my stuff a second time into the new condo. Talk about a time-stealer! So the seller's agent looked at my situation with compassion and let me occupy the condo. I was confident the delay would only span a few day's time. So I started renovating the place. I put in new hardwood floors and bought new furniture. I got a new oven and some other new appliances. I spent about $10,000 getting settled in. And then I got some really, really bad news: the deal was dead. The broker failed to accommodate for some loophole in the real estate law and we couldn't do the deal. He tried again. Two weeks later it was killed a second time. I went to another broker. Ultimately, the deal was killed three times in the course of six weeks. I was still believing – even though the deal was effectively dead my faith was alive – but to say doubt wasn't attacking my mind would be a bold-faced lie.

To make matter worse, the seller was a Russian Mafioso type. He attempted to steal my keys once so I couldn't return to the condo. He confronted me in the hallway with rage in his eyes and profanity in his mouth another time. He banged on my door literally morning, noon and late at night, sent threats through his agent, and otherwise did everything he could to intimidate me. It was a bit scary at times being a young woman who felt stalked by a violent-minded man. But I kept standing on Jeremiah 32:10. What choice did I really have at that moment? I could believe God until the victory manifested. Or I could doubt His Word and take a great loss of time, money and maybe some faith in my ability to be led by the Spirit. Long story short, the deal closed. Hallelujah! But that's not the best part. Are you ready for the payoff?

At the closing table, I found out something that made my jaw drop. For all the ranting and raving this Russian Mafioso did, for all the threatening and the intimidation, for all the drama... he had actually signed the title deed over to me while I was in Nicaragua nearly two months earlier. The Lord's rhema word to me was true: the deed was signed and sealed. Now that's just amazing. But it gets even better. My realtor, who at one point turned on me and advocated for the seller, paid my mortgage for the first six week I occupied the unit before the closing. Who ever said faith doesn't pay off? When you win the battle you get the spoils.

So just remember this the next time you are believing God for something: Your faith is a substance. Some Bible scholars translate that word substance as "title deed." Believe what God has promised you. Even if doubt is coming against your mind, don't allow it to enter into your heart. Remember, whatever is born of God overcomes the world: and this is the victory that overcomes the world, even our faith (1 John 5:4). Our faith is born of God. Jesus is the Author and finisher of it. Our faith overcomes the world. Hallelujah!

Chapter 14

REJECT FEAR AND RESIST THE DEVIL

Every time you try to move forward in faith, the enemy will try to push you back with doubt, unbelief, fear and anything else he can throw your way. Now that you've built yourself up in faith, made a quality decision to trust God, and committed to defending His honor, you are well-prepared to reject fear and resist the devil at his onset (1 Peter 5:9). All you need now is a couple more Word-based weapons in your arsenal that will help you from a practical standpoint when the battle is on. You'll get those in steps 11 and 12 of your deliverance from doubtaholism. Don't skip these steps or you could fall back into bondage to the devil's lies.

Step 11: Reject Fear

Reject fear. Two magnanimously important words. We must reject fear because it is not of God. Fear is the antithesis of faith. When you feel fear begin to grip you, remember that God has not given you a spirit of fear, but a spirit of power, love and a sound mind and (2 Timothy 1:7). Henri-Frédéric Amiel, a 19th Century Swiss poet, philosopher and critic, said this: "Doubt of the reality of love ends by making us doubt everything." God is love. If we doubt Him, what can we believe? Fear causes us to doubt Love. But perfect love casts out fear (1 John 4:18). We need to get on the God side of this spiritual equation.

I used to have a spirit of fear. In fact, it was a legion of fear demons tormenting my soul. Needless to say, that made it difficult to believe God. I even doubted my own salvation. Thank God, He delivered me from this oppression and now when fear comes knocking on my door I refuse to open it. But I don't stop there. I command it to flee in the name of Jesus. You have to do the same.

Fear and doubt often travel together. Fear even makes some people afraid to believe God because they can't bear one more disappointment. At its root, the fear most Christians are battling is a fear that God's Word won't really work for them. Think about it for a minute. If we really believed God's Word, why would we ever fear? His Word admonishes us to "fear not" hundreds of times in various situations.

There are all kinds of ways fear manifests, but the

fear of believing God's Word won't work in your life has got to the be worst because it seeks to robs from you every promise in the Bible. Again, you can't walk in faith and fear at the same time.

When you sense fear coming with its tormenting tactics, don't accept those thoughts. Reject them in the name of Jesus – and do it immediately, at the onset, with your very own mouth. Say, "I resist you, fear." Talk to it. Fear doesn't flee because you think it should. Fear flees when you resist it and command it to go.

Compartments of Fear

Many Christians are still battling fear in some area of their lives, and certainly fear can come to attack at any time. The Lord showed me how fear can be compartmentalized. I used to be afraid when someone knocked on my front door, but I wasn't afraid to go to a Muslim nation alone, travel to Cuba without the U.S. government's permission, or go glacier flying in a tiny plane in Alaska.

Maybe you're the same way. Maybe you aren't scared to bungee jump but you are petrified of public speaking. Maybe you aren't scared of public speaking but you are terrified of the dark. I did some research and discovered a phobia list. There are literally dozens of diagnosed phobias. Some are common and some are so ridiculous you know it's got to be the devil.

Here are some of the ridiculous ones:

Fear of flowers
Fear of feet
Fear of numbers
Fear of ugliness
Fear of books
Fear of teenagers
Fear of mirrors
Fear of cooking
Fear of clocks
Fear of small things
Fear of large things
Fear of houses
Fear of fear

I saw a lady on TV recently and she was scared of pickles. She was on one of those daytime TV shows. Another lady was afraid of cotton balls. She said they made a noise. These fears were literally ruining their lives. You and I aren't dealing with anything so ridiculous. But we could be dealing with subtle fears that are robbing God's best for our lives, such as fear of failure, fear of lack, fear of disappointing people, fear of loneliness, fear of making decisions, and fear of rejection.

Fear is the most difficult to overcome when its influence is so subtle it's hard to trace a behavior to the root of fear. It's an invisible enemy. If you have a fear of failure, you may not even know it because your coping mechanism and your response to it is subtle. It has become part of your personality. When fear influences you, you take action based on your fear instead of based on your faith. So you keep failing because you don't have the faith to succeed. You won't make a decision because you're afraid you didn't hear from God. You won't try to make new friends because you're afraid of rejection. You won't sow because you fear lack.

The Fear of the Lord

There is one answer to ridding yourself of the devil's fear: Fear the Lord. The Holy Spirit told me this: When you have a healthy fear of the Lord, you become so consumed with pleasing Him – you become so full of faith in His power – that there is literally no room for the devil's fear tactics. We won't take thought to his suggestions because we believe God! I'm scared not to believe God! We need to be scared not to believe God.

Fear is part of the curse of the law – Jesus redeemed us from the curse of the law. God has not given us a spirit of fear, but of power, love and a sound mind. Fear dilutes your power, causes you to doubt God's love – that perfect love that casts out fear – and makes your mind unsound.

Reverent, worshipful fear of the Lord carries a revelation of the love of God. It carries a revelation of the power of God. It carries a revelation of the truth of God's Word. It's all wrapped up in the fear of the Lord! Let's look at Psalm 112:

> Praise ye the Lord. Blessed is the man that feareth the Lord, that delighteth greatly in his commandments. His seed shall be mighty upon earth: the generation of the upright shall be blessed. Wealth and riches shall be in his house: and his righteousness endureth for ever. Unto the upright there ariseth light in the darkness: he is gracious, and full of compassion, and righteous. A good man sheweth favour, and lendeth: he will guide his affairs with discretion.
>
> Surely he shall not be moved for ever: the righteous shall be in everlasting remembrance. He shall not be afraid of evil tidings: his heart is fixed, trusting in the LORD. His heart is established, he shall not be afraid, until he see his desire upon his enemies. He hath dispersed, he hath given to the poor; his righteousness endureth for ever; his horn shall be exalted with honour. The wicked shall see it, and be grieved; he shall gnash with his teeth, and melt away: the desire of the wicked shall perish.

Can you see it? When we fear the Lord, we'll be blessed with wealth and riches and everlasting righteousness. When we fear the Lord, we will not be moved, we'll be exalted and we'll watch our enemies – including fear – flee. When we fear the Lord, we will not be afraid of evil tidings. When we fear the Lord, we would never dare to doubt Him. Hallelujah! That's good news.

King Solomon said it like this:

> "Let us hear the conclusion of the whole matter: Fear God, and keep his commandments: for this is the whole duty of man" (Ecclesiastes 12:13).

One of His commands us not to fear fear, but to fear Him. Here is a prayer you can pray over yourself to help you with the appropriate fear of the Lord: "Teach me thy way, O Lord; I will walk in thy truth: unite my heart to fear thy name" (Psalm 86:11). Amen and amen.

Step 12: Resist the Devil

Now that you've submitted yourself to God, resist that old doubtful devil whenever he rears his ugly head and he will flee from you (James 4:7). Resisting the devil also means resisting anything that comes from the devil, whether it's sickness, doubt, fear or any other ungodly thing. When doubt comes, speak to it out loud. As said before, you need to say out of your very own mouth, "I resist you doubt. I choose rather to believe the Word of God." And tell the devil, "It is written..." It may seem like it didn't work the first time. If you don't get the results you want, then hit the devil again. The really cool thing about telling the devil what the Word says as you wield the sword of the Spirit is that hearing yourself speak the Word will build faith in you. If you don't start out believing what you are saying, you will soon enough if you persevere in confessing the Word. Think about it: Your faith will grow, and the devil will get so tired of hearing you quote Scripture he'll go bother somebody else. Bye bye, doubt!

Let me leave you with a little anecdote I read from the July 2003 issue of Esquire magazine. It really drives home the impact that doubt has on what we are able to do – and what we are not able to do. As the story goes, in 1970 a Russian weightlifter named Vasily Alexeyev became the first man ever to clean and jerk 500 pounds. Arnold Schwarzenegger, the then future Mr. Universe, witnessed the feat and recalled story to an Esquire reporter: "Alexeyev asked for 499," he said, "because the psychology of 500 pounds screwed up all the weightlifters. He lifted it. But when they weighed it, they found it to be 501 and one half. That same year six guys lifted over 500."

Alexeyev did what other men, even Alexeyev, doubted he could do.

So remember what the Lord told me: Doubt is the doorway to unbelief. And if doubt is the doorway to unbelief, then faith is the doorway to God's promises.

Choose the ever living water of faith over the tumbler of doubt and receive everything God has planned for your life – no doubt about it!

Chapter 15

THE 13TH STEP

You are now free from doubt. But I'd be negligent if I didn't leave you with a 13th step. This step can save you a lot of heartache and trouble. This step can preserve your prayer requests. This step can be the difference between the life and death of your dreams. The 13th step is this: Keep your mouth shut. Let me explain. If you find yourself in a position where you are reeling from circumstantial evidence that's hurling doubtful disputations, fearful threats and imaginable imaginations at your mind and you can't seem to find a Scripture to war with, then just keep your mouth shut.

It's far better not to say anything at all than to say something contrary to the Word of God. It's better to remain silent than to confirm to the devil that he's got you in a corner with his fiery darts. Remember what your mother said, "If you can't say anything nice, then don't say anything at all." That motherly wisdom could keep you from opening the door to receive whatever the devil is trying to deliver to the doorstep of your mind. Remember, the battle is in the mind. Whatever you accept in your mind and speak out of your mouth has life to it. The power of life and death is in the tongue (Proverbs 18:21).

When Silence is Golden

I'm a big proponent of speaking the Word in every situation. We must call those things that be not as though they were (Romans 4:17). But I'd be lying if I said I've never been blindsided by an enemy attack that left me reeling for a few hours (or even a few days) before I was able regroup and counter with the Sword of the Spirit.

The truth is if a WWF wrestler sneaks up behind you, body slams you to the mat, and puts you in a figure four, you are going to find yourself a little disoriented and displaced. It may take you a minute to gather yourself, get back up and wrestle him down. While you lay on the mat, you may be tempted to talk about the pain, the injustice, the whys behind what happened. That's the worst thing you could do. In your compromised, vulnerable position you are in danger of speaking what the devil is suggesting to your soul, getting into agreement with it, and unknowingly setting the stage for another demonic blow. Remember, we don't wrestle against flesh and blood – but we do wrestle (Ephesians 6:12). You'll pin that devil down for the three count every time if you stay focused on Christ instead of doubting your authority in Him through the voice of your soul.

It was Job who said, "I cannot keep from speaking. I must express my anguish. My bitter soul must complain" (Job 7:11 NLT). Few could blame Job for complaining. The devil snuck up behind him, killed his family, stole his wealth and destroyed his health in a mere instant. But the devil was having a field day tormenting him day and night as he meditated on his dire situation. Job's prayers were prayers of despair. He was anything but silent, and his mood only grew worse. He wanted an explanation from God. He questioned God's justice. He wanted to die. It wasn't until Job repented and got into agreement with God in the matter that things began to change for him. God used Job's words of agreement to bring him out of his dire situation. God will do the same for you, no matter how deep a pit you've dug with your doubtful words.

Maybe it's not an attack. Maybe God is doing something new in our lives or in our church and we just can't see how it's possible. Maybe we're stuck in our ways, or maybe we just don't see ourselves – or Jesus – from the right perspective. It could be that what God has said is so spectacular that it defies nature. That's the situation Abraham faced when God promised him a son in his old age. When we are reeling from satanic attack or personal hurts – or when God is doing a new thing we can't wrap our minds around – that's when silence is golden.

My Mouth Shall Not Transgress

King David put it this way: "I am purposed that my mouth shall not transgress" (Psalm 17:3). Sometimes refraining from transgressing demands refraining from speech. In other words, sometimes we just need to shut up. Therein lies the challenge. It can be difficult to just keep your mouth shut in the midst of warfare or change. Zachariah remained speechless the whole time Elizabeth was pregnant with John the Baptist because he expressed unbelief in God's plan for his family. The angel had to make sure Zachariah's unbelieving mouth didn't work against God's plan. We might wish at times that an angel would strike us mute and unable to speak until the day God's prophetic word is fulfilled in our lives. But that's not likely to happen.

You are the prophet of your own life. The words you speak have power. If you speak words of doubt and unbelief, you'll get what the devil wants you to have. If you speak words of faith, you'll get what God wants you to have. It's really that simple. By your words you are justified and by your words you are condemned (Matthew 12:37). It's about what you believe in your heart and confess with your mouth – whether that's God's plan or the devil's plan. There is no such thing as believing in nothing and there are only two kingdoms to choose from: light and darkness. God isn't likely to send Gabriel to shut your mouth, but you can pray for help.

The psalmist once prayed, "If I do not remember thee, let my tongue cleave to the roof of my mouth" (Psalm 137:6). And again, "Set a watch, O Lord, before my mouth; keep the door of my lips" (Psalms 141:3). And again, "I will take heed to my ways, that I sin not with my tongue: I will keep my mouth with a bridle, while the wicked is before me" (Psalm 39:1). We don't need an angel to shut our mouths. We can pray to God, who has given us a spirit of discipline, to help us keep our mouths from transgressing.

Remember President Lincoln's words: "Better to remain silent and be thought a fool than to speak out and remove all doubt." It's better to remain silent and let the devil think you're a fool if you can't offer a faith-filled confession that's pleasing to God. But it's oh so much better to speak out the Word and in doing so build up your faith and remove all doubt.

If you can't seem to grasp the Father's wisdom – if you can't speak the Word, pray in tongues, offer a sacrifice of praise, or meditate the Scriptures due to the deluge of doubt assaulting your soul – then rely on your mother's wisdom and shut up – then run for cover. Run to mature believers who can pray with you and speak the truth to you so you can emerge from the circumstantial river with new strength to fight the good fight of faith another day. Then, when you open your mouth and speak from the abundance of your heart, there is no doubt, unbelief, worry or fear – just faith. And not just faith…faith that overcomes the world.

Prayer Against Doubt and Unbelief

Father, in Jesus' name, I thank you that your Word is true. You are not a man that you should lie. I thank you God that you've given me the measure of faith therefore I choose to believe your Word with all my heart and confess your Word with my mouth in the face of every circumstance.

I repent of allowing vain imaginations of doubt, fear and worry entertain my soul. I renounce these things and resist doubtful disputations in the name of Jesus and they must flee from me now. I thank you Lord that I can take every thought captive to the obedience of Christ and cast down those imaginations next time they come.

I thank you Lord that if I have faith and do not doubt I can command mountains and mulberry trees to be thrown into the sea. I thank you, Lord, that my faith will not fail as I confess your Word because faith comes by hearing. I walk by faith and not by sight with a faithful God. The Truth has set me free to walk in great faith and I thank you Lord. Amen.

Song – "I've Got Faith"

(Chorus)

I've got faith…
Faith to move that mountain
I've got faith…
Faith to overcome
I've got faith…
Faith to take possession.
C'mon, let's occupy at once.

(Verse 1)

I've seen the Promised Land
And I like what I see
I saw those giants there
But they're no match for me!

(Chorus)

I've got faith…
Faith to move that mountain
I've got faith…
Faith to overcome
I've got faith…
Faith to take possession.
C'mon, let's occupy at once.

ABOUT THE
AUTHOR

Jennifer LeClaire is a prophetic voice and teacher whose passion is to see the lost come to Christ equip believers to understand the will and ways of God. She carries a reforming voice that seeks to turn hearts to the Lord and edify the Body of Christ.

Jennifer serves as news editor for *Charisma* magazine, director of the International House of Prayer-Fort Lauderdale Missions Base, executive pastor of Praise Chapel Hollywood, and a board member of Christ Kingdom Evangelist Network.

Jennifer has a powerful testimony of God's power to set the captives free and claim beauty for ashes. She shares her story with women who need to understand the love and grace of God in a lost and dying world.

Jennifer writes a weekly column called "The Plumb Line" published on Charismamag. com. Some of her work is archived in the Flower Pentecostal Heritage Museum.

Jennifer is a prolific author who has written several books, including "The Heart of the Prophetic," "A Prophet's Heart," "Fervent Faith: Discover How a Fervent Spirit is a Defense Against the Devil," "Did the Spirit of God Say That?," "Breakthrough," "The Spiritual Warrior's Guide to Defeating Jezebel," and "The Making of a Prophet." Her materials have been translated into Spanish and Korean.

Visit Jennifer online at:

www.jenniferleclaire.org

www.facebook.com/propheticbooks

www.twitter.com/propheticbooks

www.youtube.com/jnleclaire

A Prophet's Heart

Have you ever wondered how false prophets become false prophets? Why are so many well-known preachers falling into sin? Can we blame it all on Jezebel?

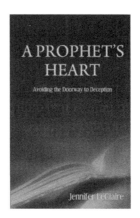

In A Prophet's Heart, Jennifer equips you to:

- Recognize false prophets
- Withstand the pressure that comes with true prophetic ministry
- Understand how the Holy Spirit warns us
- Steer clear of deception that shuts out the truth
- And much more!

The enemy seeks to pervert prophetic voices at every turn – but he can only use what's in us. Whether it's the spirit of Jezebel, pride, greed or some other issue, prophets and prophetic people need to be aware of the doorways to deception. I don't believe false prophets start off as false prophets. I believe they start off on the right track. Unfortunately, some genuine, God-called prophets end up on the road of deception. Don't let that be you! And don't get taken advantage of by false prophets!

Fervent Faith

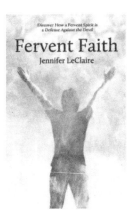

Get a new perspective on spiritual warfare and make the devil flee every time. Are you tired of spiritual highs and lows? Weary of the devil's attacks? You don't have to walk in emotional or circumstantial defeat for a single moment if you maintain a fervent spirit. That's because a fervent spirit is a defense against the devil.

In Fervent Faith, Jennifer equips you to:
- Maintain a fervent spirit at all times
- Receive a fresh anointing from the Lord
- Get prayer answers in the face of spiritual warfare
- Wield your secret weapon against the enemy
- Walk in intimate fellowship with God
- And much more!

We aren't wrestling against flesh and blood - but we are wrestling. I can guarantee you this: The devil is fervent about his ministry and he's managed to impassion thousands of evil spirits – spirits that once enjoyed the very presence of the God who created them – that rejoice when your zeal wanes.

Listen, you can't wait until the war is raging to get prepared. You need to get and stay prepared at all times because you may not always know when the enemy is going to attack your finances, when he's going to attack your health, when he's going to attack your relationships—when he's going to attack whatever.

If you aren't prepared when the attack comes, the enemy is likely to get in a few blows before you are fully dressed for battle. That's not God's will for you. He already defeated the devil, but we need to enforce that victory in our own lies. If the devil can deceive us, he can gain a foothold in our circumstances.

Defeat the devil with fervent faith!

Did the Spirit of God Say That?

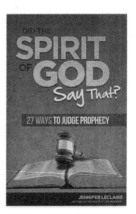

If you are like me, you love to get prophetic words. But if you put blind faith into the wrong prophecy it could open the door for the enemy to lead you out of God's will. All prophecy must be judged. But let's face it: Some prophecies are more difficult to judge than others.

That's why I wrote Did the Spirit of Say That? In this book, you'll discover 27 different ways to explore the source of a prophetic word so you can discern what spirit is really speaking. You'll learn:

- How to sharpen your spiritual ears to God's voice
- How to discern the spirit behind a prophetic word
- How to respond to false or erroneous prophecy
- How to recognize Jezebel's prophecies
- How to steer clear of prophetic merchandisers
- And much more!

Did the Spirit of God Say That? is filled with Scriptures and practical examples of real-life good, bad and ugly prophecies. Think of this as a reference guide to help you avoid the pitfalls of personal prophecy so you can hold fast to that which is good.

Breakthrough!

If you've been praying for a breakthrough, this book is for you.

In Breakthrough!, Jennifer outlines the seven principles Paul shared with Timothy in his swan song letter. This practical teaching blends Scripture, inspirational quotes, and real life experiences that encourage you to build biblical habits that transform your life—and get rid of destructive habits that are robbing your victory.

Jennifer speaks from painful losses—and thrilling wins. Abandoned with a two-year-old baby, Jennifer spent time in jail for a crime she didn't commit, then lived on food stamps for nearly a year before she discovered how to live in victory. Today, she is debt-free, healed, and walking in her calling.

God is no respecter of persons. What He did for Jennifer, He'll do for you. This book empowers you with action exercises at the end of each chapter to guide you on the path to developing victorious Christian living habits that lead to the breakthrough you've been praying for.

Spiritual Warrior's Guide to Defeating Jezebel

How to Overcome the Spirit of Control, Idolatry and Immorality!

Leading Prophetic Voice Reveals New Insight on Defeating an Ancient Evil.

According to leading prophetic voice Jennifer LeClaire, the subversive Jezebel spirit continues to deceive many. She shows, with keen biblical insight, that Jezebel does much more than most believers thought--and that it's time to expose the deceit and defeat the spirit's insidious work.

By pulling back the curtain on this seducing principality, LeClaire picks up where other books on Jezebel leave off. She demonstrates biblically not only that the Jezebel spirit uses control as a weapon but that it is a mastermind of immorality and outright idolatry. She also gives spiritual warriors the real-world strategies needed for defeating this dark spirit in the lives of God's people.

The Heart of the Prophetic

Do you want to prophesy what saith the Spirit of God with greater authority, stronger boldness and increased accuracy? Do you want that double portion that Elisha carried?

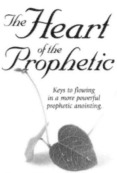

Jennifer LeClaire

Find out why Bill Hamon, Graham Cooke, Ernest Gentile, Loren Sandford and many others are raving about The Heart of the Prophetic.

Discover keys to flowing in a more powerful prophetic anointing in this no-holds-barred manuscript. Jennifer draws from her experiences to explain what it really means to operate in prophetic ministry and how to avoid the temptations that take you off the deep end. You may have read lots of books on prophecy, prophets and the prophetic movement—but until you've read The Heart of the Prophetic you haven't read the whole truth.